THE COMPLETE
Matthew Hayden
COOKBOOK

ABC
Books

Best Wishes
Jesse Campbell
Waverley College
Music Tour
2012

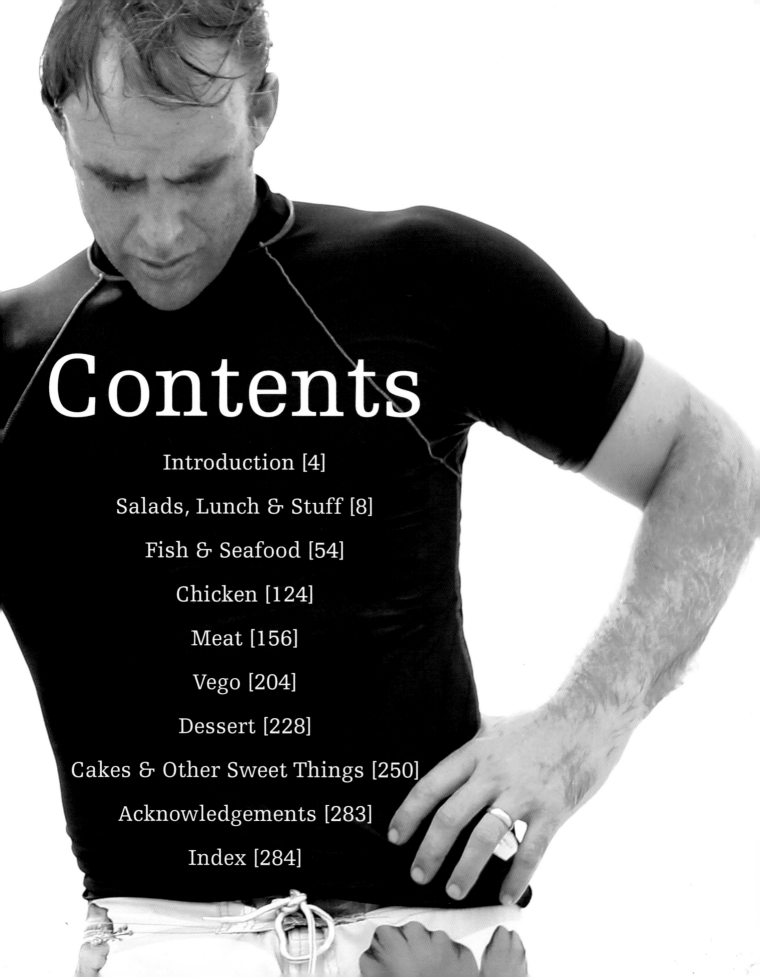

Contents

Introduction [4]

Salads, Lunch & Stuff [8]

Fish & Seafood [54]

Chicken [124]

Meat [156]

Vego [204]

Dessert [228]

Cakes & Other Sweet Things [250]

Acknowledgements [283]

Index [284]

Introduction

What incredible changes I have had in my life since releasing my two cookbooks! The most significant was the birth of our second son, Thomas. Boy, I'm so glad I have a good level of competency around the kitchen — this little bloke eats for Australia!

Then there was the announcement of my retirement from playing international cricket with Australian Cricket. The time was right for me to move to the next stage in my life and I feel a great sense of freedom in letting go on my terms and being proactive in engaging to pursue new passions and explore different horizons. However, a wonderful icebreaker occurred — the conception of the IPL and my playing for Chennai Super Kings in India. This global cricketing competition has allowed me to continue playing the game I remain passionate about and love so much, while at the same time reducing my time away from home down to two months of the year. To be able to spend quality time with my two great loves — my family and cricket is what I've strived and planned for and, thankfully, am now achieving. It is indeed a fortunate life.

I have always felt that food, cooking and the gathering of family and friends around a table for a meal is the glue in my family life and its special moments. By far the biggest hit in our family is the cutting of that special birthday cake and all the festivities that go with it. Though, the gift in itself is the fun and anticipation which comes from making tasty, nutritious delights with my three extra special, beautiful little people helping. It's the tradition of spoon and bowl licking and, finally, the enjoyment of the finished creation. Those well-prepared mealtime and after-school delicacies are always accompanied with squeals of absolute delight.

As a parent I also embrace the idea of cooking because there is a surety of the content of the food, the knowledge that the best and most nutritious ingredients are included, and the final product is good for our children and will help them to grow sturdily, both physically and mentally, and to develop good healthy eating habits. I always have that need to know what we are eating, where it comes from and how it has been prepared.

For me, cooking has been a source for exploring and developing my creative instincts but, more, it has offered me opportunities outside my work environment to extend relationships which will remain long after my international playing career is over.

Thanks to all who have really enjoyed my first two cookbooks. Sell-outs! By popular demand, they are now combined in this newly designed edition. Enjoy!

Food for thought

Kell
Grace
Josh
Tom
Idea
A couple of phone calls
Acceptances
Good recipes
Ingredients
The best produce
Creativity
Commitment
Pleasant work
Satisfaction
Preparation
Table décor
Presentation
The doorbell
Family
Friends
Fun
Laughter
Yarns
Mateship
Great food
Good wine
Relaxation
Reflection
Convivial atmosphere
Sounds of the ocean
Good attitude
Acceptance of the night
Wonderful memories
Memories that make up a lifetime
Life's story
The story is told
The story is retold
The story is passed down a generation
The story lives on
And on
And on ...

311
SPLIT GREEN
MARINATED
OLIVES

Salads, lunch & stuff

162
AI MARINATED
AUSSIE
OLIVES

309
HOT 'N' SPICY
SPANISH
BLACK

Avocado and mango salad

Up until my retirement from international cricket, I have been one of those lucky people who has had the privilege of enjoying two Christmas gatherings each year with two different, very special families – with all my relations and with my cricketing family.

Every Christmas, due to the approaching Boxing Day Test match, Kell, Grace and our relations gather in Brisbane for a Christmas lunch several days before 25 December. It is a meal that everyone contributes to in some way and my Aunty Cay's contribution is to bring boxes of takeaway chicken and make her famous avocado and mango salad. There is no better-tasting side dish than this wonderful mango salad, which is a showpiece that we like in the semi-tropics. It is hard to get a better mango or avocado than the ones offered in Queensland!

We eat till the cows come home and retreat to the pool.

Then I have my second Christmas with my cricketing family on Christmas Day. All the players' families come to Melbourne. There are mums and dads, children, wives and girlfriends.

You see your mates' lives unfolding as each year passes. You share a special time, a sacred time.

We congregate in the foyer of our hotel in the morning, then walk along the pathway by the side of the Yarra River en route to the Crown Casino where we are served an amazing meal. Father Christmas arrives and there is no question this bloke isn't Saint Nicholas. He is the real deal!

This is a prelude to the Boxing Day Test that, like the Melbourne Cup or a Bledisloe Cup Test, is a landmark day on the Australian sporting calendar.

For us, as cricketers, the week is a great celebration of what we do. You not only have Christmas but you have Boxing Day and the Test. It is a great week that I cherish.

Avocado and mango salad

You could cook the bacon and prepare the lettuce and the dressing in advance, but don't put the salad together until it's almost time to serve.

3 rashers bacon

2 mignonette lettuces

2 mangoes, peeled and cubed

2 avocados, peeled and cubed

½ cup (65 g) unsalted roasted cashews, roughly chopped

DRESSING

2 tablespoons extra virgin olive oil

2 tablespoons lemon juice

1 tablespoon French mustard

1 tablespoon thickened cream

Trim the bacon and cut into thin strips. Fry in a non-stick pan until brown and crisp, then drain on paper towels and leave to cool.

Pull the lettuce apart and wash and dry the leaves. Arrange the lettuce, mangoes and avocado in a serving dish. Sprinkle the cashews and bacon over the top.

Put all the dressing ingredients into a small screw-top jar, and shake like hell to combine.

Drizzle the dressing over the salad and serve immediately.

SERVES 10 AS A SIDE SALAD

Cucumber salad

When I was a child up on the farm in Kingaroy, we used to follow intently the progress of my Uncle Pat's greyhounds.

The Gabba dogs used to be broadcast on radio but the only place we could get good radio reception was on the tractor. Dad would drive it up a hill, pull up the radio's aerial as high as he could, tune in and listen for Pat's most famous dog. We would all gather excitedly around the tractor.

We all celebrated when the dog won and he won often! In fact, he was the Australian record holder of 21 successive wins on his home track, Cairns, hence the reason for being celebrated as The King of the North. His real name was Stationmaster, so named because my mum's father was a stationmaster on the railways.

As my cricket career evolved, I would, of course, train at the Gabba where the dogs were run every Thursday evening. It was a tradition among the boys, headed by mad punter Trevor Barsby, to have a few drinks in the dressing rooms and watch the dogs race past us as they ran around the Gabba dog track, which used to be on the outside of the boundary fence.

In 1992, Pat was down from the north on holidays, and he knew a greyhound trainer called Maureen Culey and her husband, Bernie. He also knew they had a very pretty daughter and encouraged me to meet the family after training at the dogs. So I went to meet the Culeys with Pat, and that was the first time I laid eyes on Kell.

When I started going out with Kell, I had no idea at the time I would also be given a rail's run to a delightful side salad, a cucumber salad, cultivated by her greyhound-loving mother.

Whenever we have a barbecue with Kell's mum, cucumber salad is the go!

Cucumber salad

This makes a great side salad at a BBQ.

2 telegraph cucumbers (or 4 Lebanese cucumbers)

salt

DRESSING

300 g carton sour cream

1 teaspoon grated fresh ginger

2 garlic cloves, crushed

2 tablespoons lemon juice

sweet paprika, to sprinkle

Peel the cucumbers and slice thinly. Place into a large bowl and sprinkle generously with salt. Cover and refrigerate for about 2 hours.

Squeeze with your hands to remove as much liquid as possible.

To make the dressing, mix the sour cream, ginger, garlic and lemon juice together, then stir through the cucumber. Put into a serving bowl and sprinkle lightly with paprika.

SERVES 6

Field of dreams

Growing up, we all have our dreams. As a little fella, I only ever wanted two things: to be a farmer like my dad and to play cricket for Australia. I have amazing memories of long days on the farm with Dad, sitting up beside him, helping him with the peanuts and eating lots of them, too. I can still recall the two of us coming home one day after having just had the best afternoon, playing the likes of Charlie Pride (even Kamal got a gig!) in the air-conditioned tractor, listening to his stories, and stopping every now and then to fork-in the ends of peanut rows. That day, I raced inside, covered from head to toe in red soil. Mum said later all she could see were my blue eyes. 'How good was that, Mum? I can hardly wait to be 16, leave school and become a farmer!' I was happy and thought I had my whole future 'signed, sealed and delivered'.

In time, I realised my two dreams couldn't go together. After all, there are no Test matches played in Kingaroy. But I loved my childhood home. It was fun, especially growing up with my big brother, Gary. We had all kinds of adventures.

I enjoyed my home town as well, and I still like the drive home, approximately three hours from Brisbane. My dad has cattle on his property now but, as I've said, when I was a little critter, we had peanuts. Kingaroy has the best peanuts in the world. I reckon I've tried peanuts from every country and I'm a fair judge! Thinking about it now, though, Dad should have started in the cattle industry sooner, with two hungry boys to feed. Whenever we drive home to Kingaroy, I always find myself saying to Kell: 'It makes me hungry just looking at those cows!' I've always loved beautiful fresh meat. There is nothing better than a barbeque and a cold beer on a hot summer's day.

Who knows where our dreams can take us? I'm sure at this stage, our daughter Grace thinks she is going to be a ballerina for half her life and a skateboard rider for the other half. I'm hoping that turns into surfboard riding and I can travel the world with her. (Only kidding, Kell!)

Joshua is destined for the field of science. His little mind just can't get enough information on frogs in particular, however he's into almost anything that swims or crawls across our planet.

As for our youngest son, Thomas, at just over two years old, I think his goal is to eat his way into the record books. My mum and dad say I came into the world with a knife and fork in my hands, so perhaps it's in the genes!

And Kell? She just wants the best for all of us.

But one thing I'm sure of — with love, support, commitment, really hard work and strong determination, it is possible 'to dream the impossible dream' and to 'reach the impossible star'. I know. I've done it!

Bruschetta

There is something simply delightful about Italy and the Italians' way of life. One time when I was playing county cricket in England, Kell and I had a week or so in Italy, where the weather was warm and the people flashy and enterprising. You expect Italian women to be dressed to the hilt, trying to catch a glimpse of themselves in shop windows; but it was the men who wanted to check out their reflections and see how snappy they were looking.

People-watching is an Italian pastime, made easy by the open piazzas and cobblestone streetscapes: you can spend dreamy hours simply following your aroused senses, pricked by the aromas of freshly brewed espresso, tasting beautiful Italian ice-cream in freshly baked sugar cones. Italy is also appealing as I can move around inconspicuously, soaking up all the local specialties. From Rome to Pisa to Florence, over to the coast and then through Tuscany, where we sipped wines and soaked up the silence and the sun.

Italy is a magnificent tourist destination. For us it is the perfect place. I reckon Kell and I should have married Italians because we love Italian food! As a regular dish in the middle of the day when it was hot, we loved bruschetta with a Mediterranean salad. Italy has everything going for it: the people, the weather, the scenery, the history! But best of all, Italy is loved by us for its food – and its lifestyle surrounding food, where the after-lunch siesta halts your day and sends you into sleepy bliss.

Bruschetta

This is a very versatile dish. You can try lots of different toppings, such as marinated capsicum, goat's cheese, feta, chopped olives - the list is endless. You can't really go wrong experimenting, so have fun!

4 Roma tomatoes, diced
1 red onion, finely chopped
1 sprig basil, finely shredded
2 garlic cloves, finely chopped
salt and pepper
1 loaf ciabatta or other crusty Italian-style bread
extra virgin olive oil and balsamic vinegar

Mix together the tomatoes, onion, basil, garlic, salt and pepper to taste in a bowl.

Cut 12 thick slices from the bread. Toast under a griller until golden brown. Cool, then top with the tomato mixture.

Drizzle lightly with olive oil and balsamic vinegar, and serve immediately.

SERVES 4

Camembert dream pie

If you were wondering whether sports men and women of different sporting codes mix, the answer is yes. I once came across a wise old fella on my travels who said, 'Son, two of the most valuable assets in life are mentors and social wealth. For if ya got people to look up to, help ya learn a little quicker, and they just so happen to be people of good standing, take it from me, that's your edge.'

Personally I don't think it matters terribly much where you gather motivation, as long as every now and then you have a source. It's well known that I love rugby league and union, and I am a self-confessed surfing and fishing tragic. So when Andrew Ettinghausen (ET) called and asked if I would like to 'Escape with ET', I didn't even have to think about it. The next question was even better: 'How's South Africa sound?'

So off we went, flying first to Johannesburg for our connection to Durban, then driving for six hours to Sodwana Bay while taking in all the beautiful spots Qwa-Zulo Natal had to offer. There is nothing more exciting than a South African safari and this road trip was a cracker. It felt like the entire journey had taken no more than half an hour as we swapped every story our life experiences had given us.

Now ET, despite his heart-throb good looks, was one of rugby league's die-hard warriors — right up there as one of Australia's most capped players and the kind of player great enough to bridge generations due to his long-standing service to rugby league. I had so many expectations and so little time to find out about the man behind the man. It was time to get down to the business of trying to find a chink in this Titan's armour. ET's bravery was the test of the day and this game park was our venue. We arrived in the camp at night and it was pitch black.

'Haydos, I'll drop you off first and I'll take the car back to my camp,' ET stated.

Even though his tent was only 100 metres away, the road back there was convoluted, which would give me time to sneak up to his tent with darkness as my cover.

The plan worked. By the time ET arrived, I was crouching like a lion stalking its prey. The motor stopped and there was silence. Deadly silence! I could visualise ET, ears pricked for sounds, eyes sussing out any possible moving form. Then, in the quiet heart of Africa, I could hear him coming towards the tent. Footsteps, moving closer, closer, closer. As his fingers fumbled for the zip, I leapt out from the back of his tent and ... sprung!

Never in my life have I heard such a blood-curdling, high-pitched screech: 'AAAAAAGH!' Poor old ET! This tough rugby league player was a blubbering mass of nerves, curled up outside his tent, paralysed with fear. Great bagging material!

'I thought you boys were fearless. Goes to show it's true, hey!' I said, sinking the teeth in a little further.

'What are ya talking about ya mongrel!' ET responded.

'The bigger they are, the harder they fall!' I said, stalking off as proud as punch. Camping, safaris, animals, tents, tons of laughter and fun! A camembert dream pie, hot or cold, would have topped off this perfect safari.

Camembert dream pie

spray olive oil

8 sheets filo pastry

1 teaspoon butter

2 onions, finely chopped

1 tablespoon brown sugar

1 tablespoon balsamic vinegar

5 rashers short cut bacon

3 eggs

¼ cup (60 ml) cream

salt and pepper

200 g round of Camembert, sliced

Preheat the oven to 180°C.

Spray a 23 cm pie dish or fluted flan tin lightly with oil. Spray the filo sheets lightly with oil, and stack together. Place into the dish and trim the edges.

Bake the pastry shell for 10 minutes, until golden brown. Set aside to cool.

Heat the butter in a frying pan and add the onions, brown sugar and balsamic vinegar. Cook over medium heat for about 15 minutes, stirring occasionally, until caramelised. Cool slightly. Spread the bacon, onions and camembert into the pastry shell.

Using a fork, whisk the eggs, cream, salt and pepper together with a fork. Pour over the filling and bake for about 20 minutes, until set and golden.

SERVES 6

The pizza guy

I was sure the Kiwis finally had a plan. With one game remaining in the one-day series, we were leading 4-0 and the enthusiasts from the Land of the Long White Cloud were hoping someone, anyone, would come up with an idea to put the Aussies off their game and restore some Kiwi pride.

All was revealed the moment our 'luxurious limos' (aka the catering vans) entered the stadium. Parking outside behind the changing rooms, ready and waiting to do battle with the Aussies, was New Zealand's last hope: The Pizza Guy.

The Aussie team began telling each other pizza stories. I recalled, lightheartedly, how after a heavy loss to Queensland, Victoria's dietician had asked each of the players in the losers' dressing room what he had eaten the night before.

Dean Jones had replied: 'Just a small plate of spaghetti and, er … some of those other healthy options that were provided.'

Next, Merv Hughes faced the human lie detector. 'Now, Merv, what about you?' asked the dietician. 'Me?' answered Merv in a quietly muffled tone as if butter wouldn't melt in his mouth. 'I only had a family pizza.'

'Yes,' nodded the dietician, who had picked up on the 'pizza' but not on the 'family'. 'And how many pieces of that did you have, Merv?'

'Well, that depends,' said Merv as he pulled off his smelly socks and leaned back, fully relaxed. 'What do you mean, depends?' replied his inquisitor.

'Depends on how many pieces they cut it into!'

After that story, our thoughts returned to The Pizza Guy as one Aussie player after another said: 'That's it!', 'The Kiwis are attacking our stomachs!', 'Of all the low acts.', 'Only a Kiwi!'

First, The Pizza Guy deployed smoke-screen tactics as he cranked up New Zealand's first mobile wood-fired pizza service. The Kiwis had done their homework well, as usual, attacking our lungs, a massive area of concern for me personally as I had only just got my nose across the line to tour after being struck down with pneumonia and pleurisy. The second wave of attack came soon after, as swift and precise as the first. The aroma of freshly baked pizza wafted in and around the changing room – an unbearable, tantalising, distracting scent!

Now, the Australian cricket team strongly believes that the best form of defence is attack. It just so happened that I was a non-player that day, ruled out with extensive oedema around the soft tissues surrounding the acromioclavicular joint and distal third of the clavicle, predominantly within the subcutaneous fat, extending laterally and distally over the outer margin of the deltoid muscle. In other words, I was laid low with a bloody sore shoulder. I was pretty much useless for anything apart from finding out about our latest opponent. The boys wanted The Pizza Guy's scalp or, at the very least, a few pizzas slung their way. In no position to argue, I ventured into enemy territory.

The Pizza Guy was certainly running a well-oiled unit: a state-of-the-art mobile pizza oven that had been imported from Germany. He was punching out a pizza every 30 seconds. I knew a deal had to be made swiftly so I confidently ambled up to him and started talking, sprinkling a few good Aussie words here and there to help him identify me.

'Mate, if you let me cook half a dozen pizzas, I'll supply the toppings. I'll even let you come into the Aussie change rooms for a few beers and take a few snaps showcasing your business. What do you reckon? Fair enough?'

'Done,' he replied.

How easy was that? Now he was working for us. A win-win situation. To quote from Sun Tzu, the ancient Chinese philosopher of war who regularly pops up in coach John Buchanan's pre-game team-meeting notes, the definition of true excellence is 'to plan secretly, to move surreptitiously, to foil the enemy's intentions and baulk his schemes so that, at last, the day may be won without shedding a drop of blood'.

The Pizza Guy had been given a better offer and, as per the promise, I made the pizzas and delivered them fresh to our change room, a stone's throw away, to be enjoyed after a record-breaking 5-0 series win to Australia. As any full-blooded Aussie would say: 'You bloody beauty!'

Prawn pita pizza

1 cup (250 g) crème fraiche
½ cup (90 g) sundried tomatoes, drained
lime juice, to taste
salt and pepper
4 large pita breads
500 g peeled banana (or medium) prawns
1 red onion, finely sliced
capers, optional
extra virgin olive oil
salt and cracked black pepper
torn basil leaves

Preheat the oven to 220°C. If you have a pizza stone, place it in the oven to preheat. Combine the crème fraiche and sundried tomatoes in a food processor, season with a squeeze of lime juice and salt and pepper to taste. Process until smooth.

Lightly flour the underneath of the pita breads. Spread the sundried tomato paste onto the pita breads, and top with prawns and onion. Place into the oven (on pizza trays if you don't have a stone), and bake for 10 minutes, until the prawns are cooked through and the bread is golden brown and crisp.

To serve, scatter capers over, if using, and drizzle with olive oil. Season to taste and top with basil leaves. Serve immediately.

SERVES 4

Straddie pizza

When you walk down the street in a place like Old Delhi in India, it is like winding the clock back 100 years, or even more. Early in 2004 while on tour, I walked through the centre of town and looked around in the early evening. I saw no cars, just pushbikes and ponies. And there on the footpath outside his shop was a shopkeeper with a single naked flame as his only light. He was selling fruit and vegetables. When was the last time you saw anyone in Australia living by candlelight?

How to maintain food with a chronic lack of electricity – leading to a lack of refrigeration – has always intrigued me. In the olden days in Australia, food was salted or smoked to preserve it. Well, those days still exist on the subcontinent.

In terms of flavour, nothing has changed in centuries. The same spices that were traded in very early times are still being used. The supreme taste of cold smoked meat or fish drives my desire to set up my own smokehouse. When I travel to cities around the world and I taste food that has been preserved without refrigeration, it is a constant reminder that one day I want a cold-smoker.

Straddie does have its own smokehouse, an old-style smokehouse at the local butcher's. There you can buy smoked legs of ham that are just divine on a pizza! Prosciutto is excellent on pizza, as well. And how I love eating prosciutto! It is a tasty food I come across frequently in Europe. As Kell and I have become more widely travelled, prosciutto and olives are two things we love to eat, particularly in Europe. Pizza laden with prosciutto, ham, bacon and olives is perfect for my life at home as well, and particularly when I am training because it can be eaten on the run, hot or cold.

Then again, if I am having some down time between tours – which for me usually falls in the winter months – then it is perfect served warm and eaten with a nice beer watching the footy. Believe me, when you have lived with Jimmy Maher, my Queensland Bulls team-mate, for four years, and you don't know how to make a pizza, you are in trouble. You can throw ingredients on a pizza base, put that in an oven for 15 minutes and Bob's your uncle!

Plus it also has the advantage of being eaten with your hands. I have always had a theory that any meal you grasp with your fingers is a good meal.

Straddie pizza

TOMATO PASTE

⅓ cup (50 g) pine nuts
1 cup (150 g) drained sundried tomatoes
2 tablespoons oil from the tomatoes
2 garlic cloves, chopped

PIZZA DOUGH

7 g sachet dry yeast
½ teaspoon sugar
1 cup (250 ml) lukewarm water
2½ cups (375 g) plain flour
½ teaspoon salt
2 tablespoons olive oil

200 g thin slices prosciutto, chopped
200 g sliced leg ham, chopped
1 red onion, halved and finely sliced
1 red capsicum, cut into thin strips
1 cup (150 g) pitted Kalamata olives
200 g goat's cheese, sliced
olive oil and balsamic vinegar, to serve

To make the tomato paste, put the pine nuts into a dry frying pan and cook over medium heat for about 3 minutes, until golden. Stir occasionally and be careful not to burn them. Put the sundried tomatoes, oil, garlic and pine nuts into a food processor and process to a rough paste.

Preheat the oven to 220°C.

To make the pizza dough, combine the yeast, sugar and water in a small bowl, and leave to stand for about 10 minutes, until the mixture is bubbly on top.

Sift the flour and salt into a large bowl and make a well in the centre. Pour in the yeast mixture and the oil, and mix with a wooden spoon, and then your hands, to a soft dough.

Turn out onto a lightly floured surface and knead the dough for about 5 minutes, until smooth (put more flour on the work surface as needed). Divide the dough into two portions, and roll each one out to about 30 cm round, to fit a lightly greased pizza tray. Bake for 5 minutes, until just half cooked.

Remove from the oven and, using the back of a spoon, spread tomato paste onto the pizza bases. Arrange prosciutto, ham, onion, capsicum, olives and goat's cheese on top. Bake for 15 minutes, until the base is crisp.

Drizzle extra virgin olive oil and balsamic vinegar over the pizzas just before serving.

SERVES 4–6

Cheese risotto

It's fair to say that while one of my first meals with Kell was a big hit, the venue definitely wasn't.

With my brother, Gary, his wife, Alex, and their two dogs, Kell and I went camping next to some obscure beach in northern New South Wales. Kell was taken by this meal I cooked – a chicken baked in the coals of a fire, after digging a hole in the sand and placing it into the ground. But she wasn't so sure about the camping!

I pulled up in my old army-green Kingswood with no tent – just a tarp, which I tied to the rear-view mirror and the limbs of a couple of trees. While Gary and Alex had a two-man tent, I don't think Kell was very impressed with her sleeping quarters!

She brought a doona with her and claims, 'Thank goodness I did. It was all I had to keep me warm – that and Gary's two dogs that snuggled up next to me!'

Though she had not known me for long, she was adamant about camping. 'No! No! No thanks – no camping!'

But she tried again. This time it was just Kell and I who ventured onto the northern NSW coastline. It rained solidly for four days!

'I didn't even get out of the tent for four days!' Kell tells people. 'When Matt was putting the tent up he cut off some lantana bush. While he was out surfing the ranger came around and gave me an earful for destroying the bush land! Having copped a tongue-lashing from the ranger, and enduring four days of rain, I packed the gear up while Matthew was out surfing and, when he returned, said it was time to leave. I have never been camping again!'

My cooking evolved from the bush camping days, and one of Kell's favourite meals now is a cheese risotto that I first whipped up for her one day in Melbourne while on tour in Australia.

Cheese risotto

This is a lazy risotto, rather than the traditional labour-intensive risotto which is continuously stirred. Sit down and relax with a glass of wine while it cooks!

1 tablespoon olive oil

1 large onion, finely chopped

2 garlic cloves, crushed

2 cups (440 g) arborio rice

1 cup (250 ml) white wine

3 cups (750 ml) chicken stock

1/4 cup (25 g) grated Parmesan

50 g goat's cheese or goat's feta, chopped

1/2 cup (50 g) grated tasty cheese

salt and pepper

4 thin slices prosciutto, grilled until crisp

Heat the oil in a large saucepan. Add the onion and garlic and cook until soft and lightly browned. Add the rice and cook, stirring, over medium heat for 3 minutes or until the rice turns clear.

Pour over the white wine and cook for about 5 minutes, until mostly absorbed. Add the stock, cover tightly and cook over low heat for 10–15 minutes, until the liquid is all absorbed.

Stir in the cheeses, put the lid back on and allow to stand for 2–3 minutes, until the cheese has melted. Season with salt and pepper to taste.

Serve the risotto straight away, with prosciutto crumbled over the top.

SERVES 4

Smoked ham and pumpkin soup

An unknown fact about my world record-breaking 380 in Perth in 2003 was how a good old-fashioned serving of smoked ham and pumpkin soup sustained me as an evening meal.

I had been in Perth for a week prior to the first Test against Zimbabwe. When in Perth, my body clock always seems to be constantly recovering because of the two-hour time difference. So the way I was feeling, a light meal at night really hit the spot for me.

Early days into my stay at the Hyatt Hotel, I ordered this smoked ham and pumpkin soup that came with the freshest of bread rolls. As the week progressed, I got more and more into that soup. I had it almost every day during my Perth stay. This speaks for itself, given that I felt good enough and had enough energy to bat for 10 1/2 hours. I just liked the way the soup made me feel. It was just enough and I really enjoyed this food in what was an amazing week for me.

People think a cricketer's day is over when he walks off the field. But you have to stretch, have physiotherapy and, at times, even a massage. I had a really sore back at the time and would receive physiotherapy for an hour after each day's play. Then I would have a massage for an hour. By the time I returned to my room, it was nine o'clock at night. I certainly wasn't on fire after that; all I wanted to do was simply crash out. I was just cooked! The last thing I wanted to do was go out to eat. So I stayed in, with my smoked ham and pumpkin soup.

I love soup at the best of times – from a clear soup, to a thick, stodgy one. It is especially good in the cold winter months. I enjoy that type of eating. It makes you full, but not too full.

Butter and cream are not always necessary in soup – it can easily be lightened with yoghurt, which is a healthy alternative, too. The Hyatt's soup during my stay was just perfect! Having it each night had nothing to do with superstition – it just made me feel right. And the rest is history.

I hope you enjoy my interpretation of this delicious soup.

Smoked ham and pumpkin soup

A cold night, some good company, and this delicious soup slides right down.

1.5 kg butternut pumpkin, peeled and chopped

300 g potatoes, peeled and chopped

2 teaspoons olive oil

1 small onion, finely chopped

2 garlic cloves, crushed

1 teaspoon chopped rosemary

100 g smoked ham, diced

1 cup (250 ml) chicken stock

salt and pepper

3 tablespoons milk

1 teaspoon butter

4 slices prosciutto, grilled until crisp

extra virgin olive oil, to drizzle

2 teaspoons chopped parsley

Cook the pumpkin and potatoes in a large saucepan of boiling salted water until soft.

Meanwhile, heat the oil and cook the onion, garlic and rosemary in a frying pan until soft and lightly golden.

Drain the pumpkin and potato, then place the pumpkin and half the potato into a food processor or blender along with the onion mixture, diced ham and stock. Blend until thick and creamy. Season to taste, and transfer to a saucepan to reheat.

Put the rest of the potato into a bowl and add the milk and butter. Mash until creamy, and season with salt and pepper to taste.

Ladle the soup into serving bowls and add a dollop of mash to the middle. Top with the grilled prosciutto, drizzle with extra virgin olive oil and sprinkle with parsley.

SERVES 4

The Baxter recipe for success

Picture this: It was a gloomy, overcast day in Edinburgh, Scotland — and the dark clouds were not only outside. We had just drawn the third Test but the Poms were all over us like festering chickenpox and gaining momentum in the Ashes series. The weather bureau was forecasting continuing rain, and we had a one-day international against Scotland scheduled. Whatever the weather, this was to be my game off and my good friend Allan Lamb had invited me to go salmon fishing with him and his son,

Richie, at Gordon Baxter's private 'beat'. The Baxters of Speyside have three royal warrants to their name and create wonderful soups, jams and preserves for which they have become world famous. They also lease a magnificent portion of the River Spey, home of some of the best salmon fishing in Scotland. But I had no way of getting there, so I was stuck in my hotel room, sad, sorry and disappointed.

Then the phone rang. It was Gordon Baxter, president of the company. Having heard of my dilemma, he had organised transport for me to the Scottish Highlands. I soon found myself travelling through one of the most beautiful places in the country.

The tiny Morayshire village of Fochabers is a picturesque place, with the majestic river rushing down from the misty Grampian Mountains, running through cattle-grazing land on its race of 172 kilometres to the Moray Firth at Spey Bay.

At my destination there was another sight to behold: Lamby! He looked absolutely resplendent, like a 'good sort', in the traditional, full-tartan Scottish outfit, complete with all the trimmings. He could see by the smirk on my face that I was ready to rip into him with a good old Aussie dig.

'Just look at you, you big …! You've changed; I know you have!'

'Naaah!' he laughed, as only Lamby could. 'Ya big wallaby!'

I first met Lamby when I captained Northamptonshire and he is very much a part of my extended cricketing family.

Then the competition was on. When I'm fishing with Lamby, I can't resist trying to get one up on him and this was definitely my day. Did I give him grief! The excuses rushed out of his mouth almost as fast as the River Spey raced by. 'Can't see!', 'It's raining!', 'Too slow!', 'Too low!'

At last it happened. A bite. I had actually thought Lamby was taking me down and I had not been impressed but I need not have worried. There is a traditional ceremony associated with catching your first Spey fish. They call the first one the 'virgin' fish and the fisherman is said to have 'lost his virginity'! The virgin fish is killed and blooded. Then the dead fish and the blood are smeared over the catcher's face. It's all part of the experience and I joined in the laughter and fun. Much to Lamby's disgust, I went on to hook a second fish. More ribbing for poor old Lamby. He didn't catch a single fish that day.

I will remember Gordon Baxter for the rest of my life, and not only because he shares my love for cricket and good, wholesome food. He gave me a special day in my friendship with Lamby as well as the amazing experience of fishing for salmon on the River Spey. And there is more. At a sumptuous buffet lunch, Gordon allowed me to savour some of his delicious, homemade Scottish culinary delights, and he has given me permission to share with you a Baxters recipe for salmon quiche.

Maybe we can all learn something, too, from Gordon Baxter's recipe for business success: 'Try to be the best. That's the only place to be: the top of the heap.'

Baxters salmon quiche

PASTRY

170 g plain flour
110 g butter
pinch of salt
1 egg yolk
1 tablespoon iced water

FILLING

50 g butter
1 small onion, diced
1 small leek, diced
1 tablespoon fresh thyme leaves
1 tablespoon chopped chives
250 g piece hot smoked salmon
3 eggs
½ cup (125 ml) cream
½ cup (50 g) finely grated Parmesan cheese

To make the pastry, rub the flour, butter and salt together until it resembles fine breadcrumbs. Add the combined egg yolk and water and cut through with a knife until evenly moistened. Gather the dough together to gently shape into a round disc. Wrap in plastic and refrigerate for 1 hour.

Preheat the oven to 180°C. Roll out the dough to fit a 23 cm round loose bottom flan tin. Line with a sheet of non-stick baking paper, and fill with dried rice or beans. Bake for 10 minutes, then remove the paper and beans and bake a further 10 minutes. Reduce the oven to 160°C.

To make the filling, melt the butter in a frying pan and cook the onion, leek, thyme and chives until soft. Flake the salmon into the pan, then spread into the pastry case. Stand the tin on a flat baking tray.

Beat the eggs and cream together and pour over the salmon mixture. Bake for 30 minutes until set and lightly golden, then sprinkle with the cheese and cook a further 5 minutes.

SERVES 6-8

Aioli

ROASTED GARLIC AIOLI

I find the raw garlic in traditional aioli to be overpowering, so I like to roast the garlic, which gives it a sweet, mellow flavour. This makes a magnificent dipping sauce that everyone loves with chips, fish or vegetables.

1 whole head garlic

pinch salt

4 egg yolks

juice of half a lemon

2$\frac{1}{2}$ cups (625 ml) olive oil

Preheat the oven to 180°C. Roast the garlic for 45 minutes, until soft. Cool, then squeeze the soft pulp from each clove. Place all the ingredients except the oil into a food processor, and process to combine. With the motor running, add the oil slowly in a thin stream until it is all combined.

MAKES ABOUT 3 CUPS

CHILLI LIME AIOLI

This variation is particularly good with seafood.

2 teaspoons dry mustard

1 teaspoon salt

$\frac{1}{2}$ teaspoon white pepper

$\frac{1}{2}$ teaspoon caster sugar

3 tablespoons lime juice

$\frac{1}{2}$ teaspoon finely grated lime rind

2 red chillies, seeded and chopped

4 egg yolks

2$\frac{1}{2}$ cups (625 ml) olive oil

Place all the ingredients except the oil into a food processor, and process to combine. With the motor running, add the oil slowly in a thin stream until it is all combined.

MAKES ABOUT 3 CUPS

Mango chutney

We were sitting in a fine Sri Lankan restaurant when I started talking to an elderly Sri Lankan woman who spends three weeks a year visiting her family in Melbourne. I have always loved Sri Lankan mango chutney and I ventured to ask this charming lady about it, and especially about the mangoes that go in it.

Much to my surprise, she told me how disappointed she always is with the standard of mangoes when she is in Australia – how they are far and away inferior to Sri Lankan mangoes. 'I can never get a decent mango in Australia,' she said.

'I don't wish to be disrespectful,' I replied, 'but our Bowen mangoes are bigger than a grapefruit and have more flavour than any mango in Sri Lanka!'

I told her a story about my brother, Gary, and I gorging ourselves on Bowen mangoes during the Christmas school holidays back on the farm near Kingaroy. We would eat so many mangoes, we got blisters around our mouths from the acid burning our skin. And because it was hot weather at Christmas time, we would often eat mangoes in our pool – the best place for eating mangoes, I can tell you! We didn't even have to get up and go to a tap to wash our faces and hands – we would just dunk ourselves under the water!

This almost-endless production line of mangoes came from one of my uncles, Tom. (Like another of my uncles, Pat, Tom was a Catholic priest who spent a lot of time in the communities of Bowen and the Diocese of Cairns. Both men have given years of service to the Catholic community in North Queensland.) If Tom didn't happen to visit over the Christmas period then, without fail, he would send down Bowen mangoes by the boxful. Gary and I would eat them until the cows came home! Tom's Bowen mangoes were – and still are – the finest mangoes I have ever tasted.

To prove my point, I cut a deal with the Sri Lankan lady: 'You show me how to make chutney and I'll send you down a case of Bowen mangoes when you're next in Melbourne.'

Thus, this traditional Sri Lankan chutney has made it into my kitchen.

Mango chutney

Be very careful when you are handling the hot chutney mixture, and keep the kids well away.

2 kg ripe Bowen mangoes

3 teaspoons grated fresh ginger

2 cloves garlic, crushed

1½ teaspoons chilli powder

1 teaspoon mustard powder

½ cup (125 ml) vinegar

2½ cups (550 g) caster sugar

1 teaspoon salt

Peel the mangoes and cut the flesh away from the stone. Cut the cheeks in half lengthways, then into thin slices. Put the ginger, garlic, chilli and mustard powders into a small bowl and add 2 tablespoons of the vinegar. Stir to combine.

Put the remaining vinegar and the sugar into a large saucepan. Stir over low heat, without boiling, until the sugar has dissolved (this will take a while). Use a pastry brush dipped in water to clean sugar crystals from the side of the pan.

Add the mango and the spice mixture to the pan, and bring to the boil. Turn the heat down low, and simmer for about 1 hour, stirring occasionally, until the mixture is thick and pulpy. Stir in the salt.

While the chutney is cooking, thoroughly wash some glass jars and their lids. Put them in the oven (at about 150°C) to dry them thoroughly.

When the chutney is ready, ladle it carefully into the warm jars, and put the lids on tightly. Leave in a cool, dark place for about a month before using. The chutney will keep, unopened, for about 12 months. Once you have opened the jar, keep in the fridge for up to 1 month.

MAKES ABOUT 6 CUPS

Fish & Seafood

Bug tails with mango salsa

This salsa is rich with the flavour of macadamias and mangoes, and adds a summery flavour to our most underrated crustacean — the Moreton Bay bug.

SALSA

2 large mangoes, diced

1 red onion, finely diced

1 red chilli, seeded and finely chopped

½ cup (70 g) crushed macadamias

½ cup coriander leaves, chopped

1 tablespoon olive oil

salt and pepper, to taste

1 cup (150 g) cornflour

500 g bug tail meat

1 cup (250 ml) vegetable oil

Combine all the salsa ingredients and set aside for the flavours to mingle.

Put the cornflour into a plastic bag, and add the bug tails. Twist the opening to seal, and shake to coat the tails. Heat the oil in a large wok. Shake off the excess cornflour, and cook the tails in 2–3 batches over high heat for 4–5 minutes, until lightly golden.

Drain on paper towels, and serve immediately with the mango salsa.

SERVES 4

Roy's calamari

This must be the most expensive calamari in the world! It cost me a brand new Yamaha four-stroke motor, a Haines Hunter 'family heirloom' boat, twenty grand worth of Shimano fishing gear, and another ten grand of sound equipment – radio and depth sounders!

The day started with Roy (Andrew Symonds), Trent Butler, who was a sales rep for Mossops' Fishing and Tackle, and I setting out from North Stradbroke Island to go fishing in search of some squid and the elusive snapper off the shallow reefs. But it ended with us swimming for our lives for more than an hour, sometimes through the middle of schools of bait fish, which are notorious feeding grounds for sharks.

There would have been 150 people standing around watching at Amity Point when our vessel, after being swamped in Moreton Bay, was salvaged.

The thing about our fishing is that we like to get out on our fishing grounds at first light. No matter what type of fish we're chasing, light is crucial. First light or last light is your best chance, regardless of the moon and tide times. We were out before sunrise and were sitting on the bar that runs alongside North Stradbroke Island. There was a dropping easterly swell. The plan was to cross the bar as soon as there was enough light.

Then it happened! We almost got out through the bar when we were hit pretty hard by a wave we didn't see until too late. It came down heavily and buried the back of the boat in the water. The motor cut out! I ran down to the back of the boat to see if the battery had been dislodged and – wham! – another wave hit us. Hard! And then we were right in the impact zone. That last wave turned the boat on its side and then – bang! – the next wave! The cabin was half filled with water in the blink of an eye. Our life jackets and our EPERB emergency beacon were going under, along with our hope.

Without wasting words, and with a ton of burley washing into the ocean with us, I said, 'Boys, we're swimming!' None of us wanted to be shark bait!

In the rush, we didn't even have time to put on our life jackets, but I managed to stuff my beloved sunglasses down my Speedos. We left everything, jumped off the back of the boat and started swimming with the current because there was absolutely no point fighting it. The current was taking us along the shoreline and we were about 1 kilometre off the mainland. I reckoned we had about 40 minutes of swimming in front of us.

I knew Simmo was a strong swimmer and I knew I was. We didn't know about Trent though, but he started off doing freestyle and that was a good sign. But then, after about 20 minutes into it, Trent said, 'Mate, I'm gone.' He was exhausted.

I said to him that I could swim back towards the boat, where the professional fishermen were starting to run their search patterns and alert them, or we would swim on with him doing sidestroke. I gave him a moment or two to reflect on his decision then I said, 'What do you reckon, mate, what's the go?'

'Yep, I can do it,' he said and we swam on.

We went through bait-fish schools of pilchards on several occasions but, honestly, the last thing I was thinking about was getting eaten by a shark. I was more worried about Trent and whether or not we could get him over the line.

As we approached the shore, there was another break, a lull, and then the beach break. We got across the outer bank okay and were able to stand up briefly, but then we had to swim again and Trent had no energy.

'Come on, mate, you can stand up,' Simmo encouraged.

'Just one final big push and we're home sweet home, champ,' I urged. Off we went again.

Exhaustion overcame Trent. The stress, combined with the gruelling swim, finally reached breaking point with him. Taking one arm each, Simmo and I dragged him home to safety.

Flopping down, the three of us took a moment to take stock of what had just happened. Not only were we all safe but somehow I'd managed to save my favourite old sunnies.

Suddenly, Simmo burst into laughter. 'Hey, have a look at this muppet,' Simmo said to Trent. 'Look at Haydos. He's got his sunnies on. He's bloody salvaged his sunnies!'

'Eyes and teeth, mate. God only gives you one crack at 'em!' I retorted jokingly.

At the end of the day it was a time for humour. We all still had our lives.

Roy's calamari

4 tablespoons butter

½ small onion, finely chopped

4 cloves garlic, finely chopped

3 teaspoons curry powder

500 g squid tubes, washed and sliced into rings

1 lime, halved

Melt the butter in a frying pan. Add the onion and garlic and cook until soft and lightly browned. Add the curry powder and cook, stirring, for 30 seconds. Transfer to a large mixing bowl and leave to cool.

When the mixture is cool add the calamari. Stir to coat well, then cover and put in the fridge to marinate for about 30 minutes.

Heat a BBQ plate until very hot and throw on the calamari. Cook for 2–3 minutes, until the calamari changes colour, tossing regularly.

Put onto a serving plate and squeeze lime juice over. Serve straight away.

SERVES 6–8 AS A STARTER

Chilli Mumbai lagoon crabs

I have special memories of India and Mumbai, and I may even be a bit biased towards the country, the people, the city and its cuisine because it was in India that I was able to launch my 'second' career with Australia. When we toured in 2001, the first Test of the series was in Mumbai. That was the Test when Gilly and I put on a tremendous partnership when a win looked doubtful. It was a Test we ended up winning – the only Test win of the tour!

It was so rewarding just because I was under so much pressure. To be frank, if I had not performed on that tour, I would not be playing for Australia today and I certainly would not be writing about the foods of the world.

The irony about batting in the pressure of a Test match in India is that the middle of the pitch is one of only two truly peaceful places in the country. The other is your hotel room.

In the middle of the cricket ground, you are protected from the masses by a barrier, so, aside from the eleven players trying to get you out, there is no one interfering with you. You are competing with the ball and that is all. Thus, it remains a very peaceful place.

That said, you can always hear the Indian crowd. They're always 'on fire'. The Indian crowds tend to have loud, highly pitched voices and play drums, whistles and horns. You can even smell the unique odours of Mumbai from food stalls.

The foods are quite colourful and they have chilli on everything. In India, they even have chilli on lollies. If the food does not have chilli on it, it is not an option.

I guess this is why, when you come home to Australia and have steak and chips, you miss the different flavours that enhance the food in places like India. The chilli and unique spices of the subcontinent are almost an addiction.

Your room is also a sanctuary from the teeming masses. You can just close your door to the world. But even in that room, there is a fine line. When you order room service, the waiter comes to the door along with another ten people! Everything is ten times busier. Look around you now – when you see a person, multiply that person by ten and you'll have an idea of what India is like.

Mumbai has roughly the same population as Australia in an area probably not as big as Brisbane. But it is part of the charm of the place, and your affection for Mumbai grows out of the chaos.

I asked Indian batting ace Rahul Dravid when the Indian team were in Australia, 'Rahul, what do you reckon is the big difference between Australia and India?'

He answered quite simply, 'Oh, there is so much space!'

He went on to say he could walk around town shopping in Brisbane without being mobbed. 'In India, I have not been shopping for over a decade. I can't walk around India without being mobbed, let alone shop!'

Rahul Dravid is a national hero – in India, thousands of people wait to mob him wherever he goes. Believe it or not, he said he missed the attention while touring Australia.

Reminiscing, he turned to me and said, 'I miss the affection of the people, the way they make us feel like heroes. I miss the sights, the smells.'

There is no place like home. I can vouch for that and so, too, can Rahul Dravid.

Chilli Mumbai lagoon crabs

This crab is best eaten with your hands, mixing the coconut curry sauce with steamed basmati rice. A magic meal!

4 uncooked crabs

1 tablespoon vegetable oil

2 red onions, halved and thinly sliced

6 curry leaves or 3 bay leaves

2 stalks lemon grass, white part only, finely sliced

3 slices ginger

4 garlic cloves, sliced

2 green chillies, seeds removed, finely chopped

2 tomatoes, peeled and chopped

2 teaspoons salt

1 teaspoon ground turmeric

2 tablespoons ground sweet paprika

1 tablespoon fragrant curry powder

1–2 teaspoons chilli powder

½ cup (125 ml) water

2 cups (500 ml) coconut milk

juice of 1 lime

Clean the crabs by lifting the small flap underneath and removing the shell. Pull off the gills underneath, and rinse away all the innards. Cut in half through the body, leaving the legs attached. Crush the claws slightly so the flavours can penetrate to the meat.

Heat the oil in a very large pot and fry the onions until soft and light brown. Add the curry leaves, lemon grass, ginger, garlic and green chillies. Fry for about 2 minutes, until fragrant.

Add the tomatoes, salt, turmeric, paprika and the curry and chilli powders. Stir well to combine.

Add the crabs and stir to coat in the mixture. Add the water and bring to boil. Reduce the heat to medium low, cover and cook for 10 minutes, then add the coconut milk. When it just comes to the boil again, simmer for another 10 minutes. Stir in the lime juice just before serving.

SERVES 4

NOTE

To peel tomatoes, score a little cross in the bottom and put into a heatproof bowl. Cover with boiling water and leave for a couple of minutes. Lift out, cool, then peel the skin off.

Sandcrab lasagne

2 tablespoons olive oil
1 onion, finely chopped
2 garlic cloves, crushed
1/4 cup (60 ml) white wine
400 g can diced Italian tomatoes
700 g bottle Italian tomato sauce (sugo)
1 teaspoon olive oil, extra
2 x 250 g packets instant lasagne sheets
200 g sandcrab meat
salt and pepper
1 cup (100 g) finely grated Parmesan cheese
3/4 cup (90 g) grated tasty cheese
2/3 cup (100 g) mozzarella cheese
3/4 cup (185 ml) pouring cream

Heat the oil in a large saucepan and cook the onion and garlic until soft and lightly browned. Add the white wine and then the tomatoes and tomato sauce. Simmer over low heat, partially covered, for 30 minutes.

Meanwhile, bring a large pot of salted water to the boil and add the extra olive oil. Add four lasagne sheets, one at a time, and cook for 5 minutes, until soft. Move them around with a fork while cooking to keep the sheets apart. Lift out with a large slotted spoon and plunge into cold water to stop the cooking process. Drain on a clean cotton tablecloth or tea towels.

Preheat the oven to 190°C. Take the sauce from the heat. Add the sandcrab meat and fold through; season with salt and pepper. Combine the cheeses and cream in a separate bowl.

To assemble the lasagne, layer the pasta sheets and sandcrab sauce into a large (10–cup capacity) lasagne dish. Finish with a thin layer of sandcrab sauce then a topping of the cheese mixture. Bake for 30 minutes, until golden brown.

SERVES 6

Steamed coral trout
Thai style

When I am at Justin and Sue Langer's house in Perth, I feel like I'm in my own home. For one reason or another, Kell has never been to Western Australia with me, so the Langers have been my adoptive family in the west. I am usually looking for a bit of company and I couldn't think of a better way to spend some time than with Alfie, Sue and their beautiful family of three children. Alfie loves food as much as I do. Our stomachs are often the key to our conversation. In fact, more often than not, no matter where we are in the world, Alf will make a call to the tune of, 'Hey mate, how do you make those chilli mussels again?', in the enthusiastic manner only Alf has. However, during down-time from cricket in the west, I go to their place, rest, and then eat around the dinner table like I would at home.

I sometimes give Sue a list of things to gather from the shop and I will prepare a meal, either on their outstanding barbecue or in this great kitchen they have. I come around early afternoon, while Alfie and Sue go about their normal business, and prepare a meal.

Fortunately, Western Australia is blessed with an incredible supply of beautifully fresh fish, in particular red emperor. However, I don't think there is a better fish than coral trout, with its beautiful white flesh and firm texture. Throw in some chilli and garlic, olive oil, wrap it in foil, put it on the barbecue and simply steam it in its natural juices. So simple – just remember not to overcook it. Barbecues can be a little tricky in controlling heat and basically the only way that you can ruin a good piece of fish is to overcook it.

The Langers' house is a perfect spot and it's always a great occasion to be there. It's not too often you get to relax and enjoy someone cooking a meal for you in your own house, but I love doing it for the Langers.

Steamed coral trout Thai style

Serve with a tomato and basil salad, and some steamed jasmine rice.

2 teaspoons peanut or vegetable oil

1 onion, halved and finely sliced

2 spring onions, finely sliced (keep the white and green separate)

3 garlic cloves, finely sliced

1 red bird's-eye chilli, seeds removed, finely sliced

1 kg whole coral trout, cleaned

400 g can low-fat coconut milk

4 cm piece ginger, cut into fine strips

handful of coriander leaves

Preheat the oven to 180°C.

Heat the oil in a frying pan and cook the onion, the white part of the spring onions, garlic and chilli until soft. Stuff this mixture into the cavity of the fish.

Line a large baking dish with foil. Lay the fish onto the foil and lift the foil up around the fish. Pour the coconut milk over the fish, and sprinkle on the ginger. Cover with foil and fold the edges together to form a tight seal. Bake for 45 minutes, until the flesh flakes when tested with a fork.

To serve, carefully open the foil and scatter the coriander and green part of the spring onions over the fish.

SERVES 4

Calypso crayfish

There is a bar on the West Indian island of Antigua called Lashings. It sits on a beach – just about anywhere you go in the West Indies is on a beach. And if you're not on the beach, then you're in the water, because that is what the West Indies is – a place of white sandy beaches and crystal-clear blue water. The bar has a wooden floor that sits half a metre above the sand. It is more or less a grass hut! I have always thought that if a strong northerly wind blew, there wouldn't be much of Lashings left.

Lashings is owned by Curtly Ambrose and Richie Richardson – two of the West Indies' finest ever cricketers. Ambrose and Richardson lured Australian cricketers for years like a snake charmer lures snakes, talking themselves up and telling Australians how good they were – and they were!

I can vividly recall the times when Curtly would amble out to a Test wicket and address only the captain. A man of a few words, he would acknowledge him with a simple 'Skipper!'.

But put a cricket ball in his hand and his focus would be only on the batsman. And as an Australian opening batsman, I can tell you it was not a pretty sight: his huge frame, relaxed and focused totally on me from the opposite end of a cricket pitch, starting his run.

And then the West Indian antics would start. Firstly, there would be a clap of hands from somewhere and a voice would say, 'Ooooh! I t'ink we're in bus'ness here, mun!' As a team, they had a distinctive way of repeating themselves, very quickly: 'Yea, mun! We in bus'ness here, mun!' That would start the ramble: 'I t'ink he wan' to hook, eh, mun!' This would be followed by laughter. Another would add, 'Get 'im on a stepladder, mun! On a stepladder!' Then, more advice: 'Waist an' chin, Amby! Waist an' chin!'

Then in would come the ball like a bullet. Crash! The 'death rattle'!

I have a very vivid memory of Curtly scattering my stumps during the Boxing Day Test. I can still see that blasted stump rolling over the deck from a ball that struck the wicket so hard it almost followed me back to the pavilion!

The West Indies thrives on music, and so, too, do the cricket spectators! There is always a carnival atmosphere at their grounds. Calypso music, bongo drums, instruments of all kinds, colourful characters, and singing and dancing can be heard from all parts of the ground. In fact, every ground has huge speakers installed on the buildings. If the West Indian cricket team records a win, especially against the Australians, the whole stadium turns into something that resembles an American hip hop night club. It's party time – big time!

That same atmosphere extends to Lashings.

Every Friday and Saturday night, Curtly and Richie can be found at Lashings – Curtly on his guitar and Richie on his drums, jamming until the wee small hours of the morning. When we were touring in 2003, the West Indies won a Test and everybody was in celebration mode. The whole beach around Lashings was packed with people as Curtly and Richie jammed away.

That's the wild side of Lashings, but it has another personality as well. Wander down mid-week, or even midday on a weekend, and it is a tranquil place where water lapping peacefully on the sand replaces the beat of Richie's drums. It's as good as it gets, with water the colour of the sky, and rich green foliage swaying around the headland.

At Lashings, Kell, Grace and I joined Steve Waugh and his wife, Lynette, for lunch. For $US25 you get these massive crayfish. West Indians love their spices, so you'll often find coloured spices sprinkled over the crayfish and a wedge of green lime on the side. Imagine, against the backdrop of the beautiful blue of the ocean and white of the sand, these gloriously painted crayfish with red tinges and white flesh, dappled with colourful spices and lime. Such contrasting colours! Magic!

Afterwards, you slide down off your chair, onto the beach and into the water like a dirty big croc. You just bask in the Caribbean sunshine. You make an entire afternoon of lunch at Lashings.

Calypso crayfish

Serve these with salad for the health conscious, or if the waistline is not an issue serve with hot chips and cold beer.

4 whole, uncooked crayfish (rock lobster)
200 g butter
1 rasher bacon, finely chopped
1 onion, finely chopped
2 garlic cloves, crushed
1 lime, quartered
splash of Tabasco sauce
salt and pepper

Chop the crays in half and clean in salty water.

Preheat a chargrill or BBQ plate until hot. Place the crayfish halves flesh side down onto the grill to sear the flesh.

Flip onto the shells for 8–10 minutes, until cooked through (the shell will turn pink and the flesh will be white).

Meanwhile, melt the butter in a frying pan and brown the bacon, onion and garlic.

Place the cooked crays onto a plate and spoon on the browned bacon and onion mixture.

Splash on Tabasco sauce and top that off with a squeeze of lime juice, to taste. Season with salt and pepper.

SERVES 4

Three men and a boat

Take a couple of good mates, a few willing (or not so willing) fish, some rods and bait – then add a boat. And there you have it – the perfect recipe for mateship.

When it comes to fishing expeditions I try to make sure I've got a few of my great mates on board, and Guy Reynolds and John Dumphy are perfect examples. We have had some great times together. You might remember them from my first book, where they got an honourable mention! Well, all of us lead pretty full-on lives – Guy runs the Macquarie Bank Sports Foundation (which I have been involved with for five years) and John is the boss of Shimano Fishing Industries in Australasia – so on the rare occasions when we manage to get together to indulge our passion for fishing, that time is golden.

Our adventures always reel in a good fishing story or two – so I've always got some yarns up my sleeve. On one particular expedition, we'd arranged to meet in Coffs Harbour, a great little town on the east coast of Australia. In a lot of ways, it's really one of those 'last frontiers'. Even though it has developed enormously and rapidly, it is still very quiet and relaxing. A little ripper of a place! The perfect rendezvous for an unforgettable fishing expedition with some good friends.

The other reason we were all meeting in Coffs was because John was there with his massive fishing boat to compete in the Coffs Harbour fishing competition. Now, believe you me, John's boat was not any old boat. It was Shimano's number one game-fishing boat, which is set up for trolling lures around and catching marlin and whatnot. It goes all over the country. We'd decided it was an opportunity not to be missed. We could catch up and take advantage of the extraordinary snapper grounds that are second to none – only a couple of kilometres off-shore, they are simply astonishing and the stuff of legend!

Once we headed out to meet the fish, it was game on! You don't get three competitive blokes together and expect them to behave! We ribbed each other about everything under the sun – and especially our various fishing techniques! Being in a boat, as well, is the best. Especially a big one! And it's always great to get out to the sea, in it, on it and around it. I love it.

As a bonus, two of the day's prized fish were a pearled perch and a 7.5-kilogram snapper that I caught. I'd love to say it … I will say it! Of course, I out-fished them all! (It's my book, I can say what I like!) That night, we took the fish to a Thai restaurant, where they cooked up the most incredible scored and wok-fried snapper and pearly perch. Delicious!

We are so lucky to have such great-quality seafood in Australia, and there's something satisfyingly primal about catching your own fish. What a great feeling, being able to do that and literally put food on the table. Just magnificent!

The banter John, Guy and I share between fish and the swells is what keeps our friendship going – even if we don't see each other for a year or more, on our next fishing adventures we can always pick up where we left off. Fishing trips like this, and many others, always provide a welcome break for me. The demands of training and touring can make it hard for you to pursue your passions outside cricket – free time is hard to come by.

Whole fried fish with two sauces

I love this fish. It has lots of texture, with the crisp skin and succulent moist white flesh around the bones. Yum!

2 cups (500 ml) olive oil

1 bunch rosemary

1 whole head garlic, broken into cloves and peeled

4 x 600 g snapper or pearl perch, cleaned and scaled

1 cup (150 g) cornflour

BALSAMIC SAUCE

½ cup (125 ml) balsamic vinegar

⅓ cup (80 ml) lemon juice

YOGHURT SAUCE

1 cup (250 g) plain yoghurt

2 tablespoons lime juice

½ cup coriander leaves

1 green chilli, seeded and finely chopped

salt and pepper to taste

Heat the oil in a large wok or heavy based frying pan until very hot. Add the rosemary and garlic. Cook for 1 minute, then remove and set aside. Working one at a time, dust the fish in cornflour and shake off the excess. Cook the fish for 4 minutes each side, until golden brown. Drain on paper towel. Repeat with remaining fish, reheating the oil each time. Serve with one or both of the sauces.

To make the balsamic sauce, place the reserved rosemary and garlic into a medium saucepan. Add the balsamic vinegar, bring to the boil and cook for 5 minutes, until reduced slightly. Stir in the lemon juice, and pour into individual bowls for dipping.

To make the yoghurt sauce, place all the ingredients into a food processor and process until smooth.

SERVES 4

Fish pie

Over in Western Australia, there is a mate of Justin 'Alfie' Langer's who supplies crayfish to the global market. Now it has become a tradition that during a Test match in the west, he comes in with a massive box of crayfish and prawns.

We sit around after a Test match, having a few glasses of wine, or some beers, and not only chew the fat, but also chew into these massive cooked crayfish, banana prawns and spotted prawns.

In October of 2003, on one of the last nights of the Test where I scored 380 against Zimbabwe, I was around at Alfie's house looking to break my run of the Hyatt Hotel's smoked ham and pumpkin soup that I had lived on as an evening meal. Alfie's mate loaded us up with all the seafood in the ocean. He brought around prawns, squid and scallops. All the boys were there – it was a feast for kings!

He also brought around this fish pie. Absolutely succulent! A beautiful meal! It had the boys lining up for seconds.

Fish pie

400 g fish fillets, cubed (red emperor is great)
200 g prawn meat
200 g scallop meat
200 g mussel meat
1 tablespoon olive oil
1 onion, finely diced
2 garlic cloves, crushed
1½ cups (375 ml) milk
2 teaspoons cornflour or arrowroot
1 teaspoon chopped fresh oregano
salt and pepper, to taste
50 g butter, melted
3 sheets filo pastry

Preheat the oven to 180°C.

Put all the seafood into a 6-cup capacity greased ovenproof dish. Heat the oil in a medium saucepan and cook the onion and garlic until soft and lightly golden. Add the milk to the pan and warm through. Put the cornflour into a small bowl and add a little of the milk. Stir to make a smooth paste, then add to the pan. Stir over low heat until thickened.

Stir in the oregano, and season with salt and pepper.

Pour the sauce over the seafood and stir to combine. Brush the sheets of filo with melted butter, one at a time, and stack together. Fold in half and lay over the top of the pie mixture. Tuck or fold in the edges. Brush with butter.

Bake for 30 minutes, until crisp and golden, then serve immediately.

SERVES 4

Green and gold all round

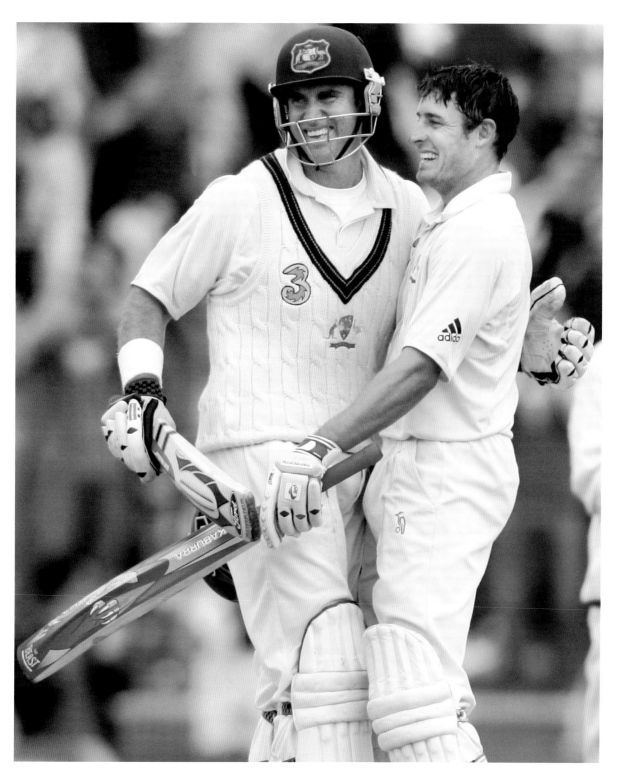

It was the second Test match, Australia versus West Indies, and a very significant one at that. I was as happy as a pig in mud since I had a front-row seat to watch Michael Hussey reach his potential on the international stage. Together, Michael and I were involved in a wonderful partnership, every batsman's dream, culminating in not only both of us making hundreds but also leading the charge in our crushing victory over the West Indies. Party time! And when Australia wins a Test match in under three days, the days off are gold – and in this case, they were 'green and gold'!

We don't always hang out together on these days off but, in true Aussie spirit, we had organised to come together that evening to watch Australia's play-off match against Uruguay to qualify for the World Cup finals.

The tasks of the day were set out: Andrew Symonds (Simmo) and Michael Clarke (Pup) were to go fishing and catch flathead (they actually did it this time too!). Ricky Ponting and I were responsible for getting other odds and ends, and bought some fresh blue-eye trevally and scallops from the beautiful little seafood markets nestled along Hobart's picturesque waterfront. And Stuart MacGill, aptly nicknamed Grape Juice, and Adam Gilchrist (Gilly) were sent on a mission to unveil Tassie's finest pinot noir.

Now, on most footy nights, an unusual tension exists. Pup, Simmo and I love rugby league, in line with the east coast tradition. Ricky is an AFL man, Tassie born and bred, and Gilly is our number one soccer fan. But on this night differences were cast aside as we'd had a solid dose of patriotism firmly injected into our veins after our demolition of the WI and, enthusiastically and excitedly, we came together as one to watch history in the making. Go Australia! Go! Sweet victory again! You beauty! Australia was off to the World Cup in Germany.

I reckon that night we had the recipe for green and gold success – great mateship, beautifully fresh beer battered flathead and one of Tassie's finest pinots: Kelly's!

Beer battered flattie

This is a wonderful summer speciality. It is great served with a green salad and some mayonnaise, or even a dollop of the yoghurt sauce on page 26. Washed down with a few cold beers while watching the cricket, of course.

1¾ cups (265 g) self-raising flour
1 cup (250 ml) beer
1 cup (250 ml) water

vegetable oil, to deep fry
4 flathead fillets (about 150 g each)

To make the batter, sift the flour into a bowl, and make a well in the centre. Gradually add the beer and water, whisking to combine. Set aside for a few minutes.

Half fill a large saucepan with vegetable oil, and heat over medium high temperature. Using one pair of tongs, dip a fillet into the batter, let the excess drip off briefly, then put into the oil. Cook for 4–5 minutes, depending on the thickness of the fillet, until golden brown. Lift from the oil with another pair of tongs or a slotted spoon, and drain on paper towels. You should be able to cook two at once, but don't overcrowd the pan.

Note: You can vary this recipe by replacing some of the flour (about ¼ cup) with chickpea flour, and adding a good pinch of your favourite curry powder.

SERVES 4

Matty's mussels

Kellie and I were enjoying the beautiful sun-drenched south of France when we came across the most succulent mussels dish we have ever tasted.

There is much travel involved during an English county season and there's only a small window of opportunity of, say, four days to break away from cricket commitment. Leaving tiresome travel between matches behind, we flew to Monaco, hired a car and drove to Cannes.

During the flight, Kellie was seated in business class and I was down the back in 'cattle class'. On arrival at Monaco airport she said to me, 'You wouldn't believe who was on our flight – Richie Benaud!'

'No way!' I said. 'Come on, Kell. You've got to be kidding! I reckon you've got him confused with someone else.'

But Kell was adamant. 'No! No!' she said. 'It was Richie.'

Anyway, I rocked up to the baggage collection and – blow me down! – there was Richie in his beige suit. 'Well, fancy seeing you here!' he said to me.

'Yeah! I thought the same actually, Richie. Kell told me you were here but I didn't believe her. So, what're you up to?'

Richie answered in his trademark manner, heavily stressing the final consonants of words. 'Just thought I'd take a little break. Daphne and I own a little unit in the south of France. Not, ah, really very big. Not big … at all really! Just, ah, big enough to swing a cat. And,' he added with a glint in his eye, 'to swing Daphne now and then! Really marvellous stuff! Really!'

It's always good to catch up with Richie. He's a top bloke and he and his wife really enjoy their breaks when they get a pause in Richie's English television commentary commitments on the BBC.

So we parted company with Richie, hired the car, and off we went.

A glorious atmosphere envelops you in Cannes. High on a hill, there is a cathedral that dominates the horizon. Narrow cobblestone streets wind, snake-like, up the hill for a kilometre. With each step you take, you feel like you're stepping on history. It's like an aura that permeates the whole place. An amazing city!

On the way up we came across this little restaurant that specialises in mussels. They serve blue cheese and honey-mustard mussels in a large pot, with a fresh French stick that you use for dipping into the cheese and mustard sauce. It is so simple and beautifully presented, and so easy to eat. There we were, eating mussels, sipping on a little French bubbly, under sun-drenched skies while the sea lapped at the shore. It was awesome!

So that is where my taste for mussels comes from.

At North Straddie, there is a local bloke, Mal Paskin, who is one of the few remaining fishmongers on the island. Whenever we're there, we stop by to pick up a couple of bags of his green-lipped mussels, throw them in the pot with some wine, tomatoes and herbs, and tuck in.

Matty's mussels

Have some hot crusty bread on the side for mopping up the delicious sauce - you won't want to waste a drop.

1 kg green-lipped mussels

1 tablespoon butter

1 onion, finely chopped

4 garlic cloves, crushed

1 red chilli, finely chopped

2 ripe tomatoes, chopped (about 300 g)

400 g can diced tomatoes

2 cups (500 ml) white wine (chardonnay or sauvignon blanc)

½ teaspoon chilli powder

salt and pepper, to taste

small handful of fresh coriander, chopped

1 tablespoon extra virgin olive oil

Scrub the mussels and pull off the beards.

Heat the butter in a very large pot and add the onion, garlic, fresh chilli and fresh tomatoes. Cook over a medium heat until soft.

Add the canned tomatoes, half the white wine and the chilli powder. Bring to the boil, then reduce the heat and simmer the sauce for 20 minutes. Season with salt and pepper.

Add the remaining white wine and the mussels to the pot. Bring back to the boil and cover with a tightly fitting lid. Steam for 10 minutes, until all the mussels have opened (discard any that don't open after this time).

Serve sprinkled with coriander and drizzled with olive oil.

SERVES 4

Pad Thai

250 g dried rice noodles
¼ cup (60 ml) fish sauce
¼ cup (60 ml) sweet chilli sauce
2 teaspoons peanut butter
3 tablespoons safflower oil
1 tablespoon tamarind sauce (optional)
3 garlic cloves, crushed
1–2 red chillies, seeded and finely chopped
1 chicken breast fillet, finely sliced
10–12 green prawns, peeled, tails left intact
2 eggs, lightly beaten
2 spring onions, finely sliced
100 g bean sprouts
½ cup coriander, chopped
½ cup (80 g) chopped peanuts
lime wedges, to serve
extra sweet chilli sauce, to serve

Place the noodles into a large heatproof bowl, cover with boiling water and soak for 10 minutes. Combine the fish sauce, sweet chilli sauce and peanut butter; set aside.

Heat the oil in a large wok, and add the tamarind sauce if using. Stir fry the garlic, chillies, chicken and prawns over high heat for about 3 minutes, until cooked through. Add the eggs and stir fry until just set and kind of scrambled.

Add the noodles and sauce mixture to the wok, and stir fry for 1 minute, until well combined. Toss through most of the spring onions, bean sprouts, coriander and peanuts, reserving some for garnish.

Serve topped with the reserved ingredients, with lime wedges and extra sweet chilli sauce on the side.

SERVES 2–3

Prawn rice rolls

If you want to make these ahead of time, place in a single layer on a tray, cover with a damp cloth and place into the fridge.

DIPPING SAUCE

2 large red chillies
2 tablespoons palm sugar
1 tablespoon fish sauce, approximately
1–2 tablespoons lime juice

FILLING

1 medium carrot, cut into matchsticks
2 stalks celery, cut into thin strips
100 g snow peas, finely sliced
2 spring onions, finely sliced
1 cup (75 g) bean sprouts
1 cup coriander leaves

15 x 22 cm round rice paper wrappers
15 large cooked prawns, peeled and halved lengthways

To make the dipping sauce, roast the chillies under a hot grill until the skin is black and blistered. Place into a plastic bag to cool then remove the skin and seeds. In a mortar and pestle, pound the chillies with the palm sugar. Add the fish sauce and lime juice, to taste.

Combine all the filling ingredients in a large bowl. Fill a shallow dish, large enough to hold a rice paper wrapper, with warm water. Working one at a time, dip a wrapper into the water and leave for about 1 minute, until soft. Drain, and place onto a clean tea towel.

Place a small handful of the filling across the base of the wrapper. Top with 2 prawn halves, then fold in the sides and roll up. Repeat with remaining wrappers and filling. Serve with the dipping sauce.

MAKES 15

Udon prawn salad

This is such a simple and refreshingly 'zingy' salad to have on a hot summer day.
500 g fresh udon noodles

1 tablespoon sesame seeds
1 tablespoon olive oil
½ teaspoon sesame oil
½ cup coriander leaves, roughly chopped
1 small red onion, finely sliced
2 spring onions, finely sliced
500 g cooked prawns, peeled
1 tablespoon lime juice
2 red bird's-eye chillies, seeded and finely chopped
lime wedges, to serve

Prepare the noodles as directed on the packet. Toast the sesame seeds in a dry frying pan over medium heat for about 2 minutes, until golden brown. Transfer to a plate to cool.

Drain the noodles and place into a large bowl. Add the olive oil and sesame oil and toss to coat. Add the remaining ingredients and toss to combine. Serve with the lime quarters.

SERVES 2–3

NOTE

You can buy udon noodles from the supermarket, either in the fridge section, or on the shelf with other Asian ingredients, vacuum packed. Preparation instructions vary, but as they are pre-cooked they usually only need to be rinsed under hot water to separate the strands.

Prawn and scallop skewers

How blessed with seafood we are in Australia and what a Mecca Darwin is for sports fishermen! It has fishing like you wouldn't believe, and a huge variety of fish. There is a perception that if you do not catch a barramundi in Northern Territory waters, then your trip is unsuccessful, but that's a statement I disagree with very strongly.

If you catch anything that moves really quickly, then you've had a victory in the NT waterways. I reckon it has the best fishing ever. And it is an adventure for every second of the day.

On a visit to Darwin during the Test series versus minnows, Bangladesh, I bumped into my long-time friend, Ben Dark, who, believe it or not, escaped from the big smoke to become a fishing local in Darwin.

'Mate, this place just gets into ya blood. You'd be hopeless, Haydos, up here. You'd never wear the baggy green again!' he said with a cheeky grin.

You look at the water and your imagination runs away with you. Your instincts take over, telling you what you could be catching and how you could be catching it. The waters are so bountiful!

A great bloke with a vast knowledge of the North is John Dumphy, who, though he lives in Sydney's Cronulla, has the best fishing contacts around. Why wouldn't he? He is, after all, the owner of Shimano Fishing Australasia and one of my great mates.

John knows a father and son, George and Ronny Voukolos, who run Fishing & Outdoor World tackle store in Darwin.

'Matt, when you get to Darwin you've gotta call in and see George and Ronny. Tell 'em I sent ya, mate. We've been friends for over 35 years and not only are they top blokes, they cook the best seafood pasta on earth.'

With a recommendation like that, how could I not call in and say g'day?

Like all people of the North, their generosity and hospitality were outstanding. Ronnie's enthusiasm for fishing (not to mention mine!) found us in a tinnie the same day I called to meet him in the tackle shop. A 4 am wake-up call the following morning saw us out again. Every day some spectacular fishing adventure happened.

You don't become one of the leading presenters on Channel 9's *Getaway* without a hunch! Ben was right. I had become that fishing junkie.

George, on the other hand, was waiting for us at home and, with the raps John had given his pasta, man, were we hungry! What a menu of seafood, with his prawn and scallop skewers done on a barbecue being one of George's specialties.

Some serious eating followed!

There's something about the water that really stimulates the appetite. Whether I am surfing, swimming, fishing, just walking along the beachfront or sitting in a restaurant beside the sea, I just want to eat!

Prawn and scallop skewers

These skewers are very simple but that is usually the best way to appreciate good fresh ingredients. Serve with rice and/or salad for a meal, or as a starter before a more substantial seafood dish.

1 kg green prawns
500 g scallop meat
½ cup (125 ml) olive oil
2 limes, quartered

Soak 12 wooden skewers in cold water for about 30 minutes before you start. This prevents them burning on the BBQ.

Peel the prawns, and leave the tails on if you like. Thread the prawns and scallops onto the skewers, alternating as you go.

Brush with olive oil and put onto a hot BBQ plate. Cook for about 1½ minutes each side, until the flesh changes colour and is just cooked. Be careful not to overcook.

Remove from the heat and squeeze lime juice over. Serve immediately.

MAKES 12 SKEWERS

Salt-crusted red emperor

Wherever I have travelled in the world, I have always taken my fly-fishing rod and fly-tier with me. And it was my fly-rod that, indirectly, led me to discovering the wonders of salt-crusted red emperor.

In Galle, Sri Lanka, I stayed on the waterfront at a magic place called the Light House Hotel that, appropriately, beamed a light into the darkness to warn ships of the nearby coastline. In the morning I went for walks along the beach, watching the locals fish along the way. It was a fascinating sight! They stood with cane poles that had a string attached to the end, and they would pull out bait fish with no matter of fuss.

If you ever went to a school fête as a child, you may recall fishing with a stick that had a string attached and a fish-hook secured to its end. There would be a pool of water filled with little tin fish. The object of the game was to use your 'fishing line' to pull up a tin fish. If you hooked a fish, you won a prize.

Well, this is like everyday fishing in Sri Lanka. The people catch what they call mackerel, but it is really bait fish. Watching them fish gave me the urge to produce my fly-rod and see what I could catch standing on some rocks next to the beach.

This was in 1999 and I had not played a Test in Sri Lanka at that stage. I was just a squad member, little known to the locals, I am sure. Within five minutes of my fishing, 100 people had encircled me. I thought to myself, 'Gee! I'm popular.' I had a great hour or so!

When I finally came down from the rocks, one of the Sri Lankans approached me and asked me to come back to his village. I thought what a friendly group of people they were and did not hesitate. But when I arrived at the village, I soon realised I was not the star attraction. My seven-weight fly-rod and my flashy flies were the centre of attention!

I bargained with one of the locals: 'Listen, mate, I'll teach you to throw a fly-rod if you teach me how to cook a fish in true Sri Lankan tradition.'

Now, by good fortune, the fellow with whom I had bargained just happened to be a chef at the hotel where we were staying. I couldn't believe my luck!

So, back at the hotel, he had the catch of the day ready to cook up. It was like a jewfish, similar to the ones you get in Western Australia, black in colour, not silver like the ones we have in Queensland. It was a magnificent fish! I told the Aussie boys to forget about the buffet that night – I was cooking them fish! 'Yeah! Sure you are!' was echoed in disbelief. So I took up residence in the kitchen and that chef taught me how to cook it.

He covered it in salt and placed it in the oven. The salt formed a hard crust on the outside, about two centimetres thick. When it was cooked, we poured brandy on it, lit it up like any top-class chef would do, and I carried it out to the waiting Australian cricket team on a big baking tray, smiling as I went.

Mind you, I had my fingers crossed. Being the tour rookie, I was desperate to save face! When the flame went out, I got my knife under the shell of salt and slowly moved it around the fish, lifting the salty crust off as I went. And then, *voila*! My beautiful steamed fish was revealed.

There were no complaints about the food that night! That evening the chef also showed me how to make a Sri Lankan seafood risotto.

Again, there was the reward for opening myself up to other people. I could have easily declined the invitation to the village and gone back into the protective cocoon of the hotel. But … look what I would have missed out on!

Salt-crusted red emperor

2 kg red emperor, cleaned

12 egg whites

1 kg finely crushed sea salt

1 red chilli, finely chopped

1 teaspoon finely chopped fresh ginger

2 garlic cloves, finely chopped

1 lime, finely sliced

⅓ cup (80 ml) brandy, optional

Preheat the oven to 200°C.

Put the egg whites into a clean, dry bowl. Using electric beaters, beat until stiff peaks form. Fold in the sea salt to form a thick paste.

Spread half the salt mixture onto a large baking tray. Lay the fish on the salt mixture, and put the chilli, ginger, garlic and lime slices into the abdominal cavity.

Spread the remaining salt mixture over the fish to enclose completely; it should be 1–2 cm thick. Place into the oven and bake for 40 minutes.

To serve, cut around the mid line of crust and remove the top. It may crumble, but just pull off in large pieces.

If you like, pour brandy over the fish and immediately light to flambé. Serve straight from the baking tray.

SERVES 6

NOTE

With the left-over egg yolks you could make aioli (see recipes on page 49)

Seafood gumbo

The northern Queensland outpost of Cooktown was the scene of one of my great fishing flops. Yet, just 45 minutes south, it was the scene of one of my great fishing triumphs. Fishing can be fickle like that.

Andrew Symonds and I were in the north on the beautiful Endeavour River on which Cooktown stands. We were definitely 'two fish out of our water'! We had fished the river hard for seven days and caught just three fish.

We had tried all the different locations, all the right baits and, believe me, had asked all the right people all the right questions.

'Ah, mate, ya shoulda been 'ere yesterday, 'eh,' we were told. But today it was deathly quiet!

There's a saying in North Queensland fishing circles: 'No Run. No Fun.' And there was no tidal run in the Endeavour River because there was no moon. The tides were really neap. It was hot, very hot, and we were tucked up on the mangroves being eaten alive by sandflies, dodging crocs and making pathetic excuses for why it just wasn't happening for us. If we had not been such good mates, we would have strangled each other!

So on the seventh day, we left for a small community 45 minutes south called Archer Point. We set up camp on the beach, just opposite an unnamed island where the grave of a lone sailor lies. (Perhaps he wasn't catching fish either!) Our tinnie had no depth sounder, so we threw the anchor out and if we hooked upon the reef, we cast out.

Then it happened! I yelled excitedly but slowly, as I spat the sixth-day dummy out at the same time, 'We're into 'em, mate!'

Simmo gave his usual snuffle and rub of the nose and said, 'Yeah! 'Bout bloody time!' Then we were running hot. Fish everywhere!

I couldn't believe it! Within 15 minutes I was sick of catching fish. I started filleting them and throwing their backbones over the side. But they were barely hitting the water as Spanish mackerel smashed into them. They were absolute horses! We had plenty of fun on those mackerel for an hour.

And then there were the queenfish. There must have been three acres of queenfish and none was less than 10 kilos. Every time we threw in, we got a fish. It didn't rain, but it poured fish. We really needed that. We had been struggling for so long on the good old Endeavour River.

Just as we had become frustrated not catching fish at Cooktown, we were almost frustrated catching fish off Archer Point! The trip was so good! All the effort we went to and could not catch a fish; then, barely trying, we were catching fish after fish. That night we lit the campfire on the beach and talked lies all night!

Seafood gumbo

Gumbo is a spicy stew which comes from Louisiana in southern USA. It is based on tomatoes and capsicums, and to be authentic would include okra. This can be hard to find, so leave it out if you have to — it will still taste great. Serve with rice to soak up the sauce.

2 tablespoons peanut oil

1 large onion, chopped

1 large red capsicum, chopped

1 large green capsicum, chopped

2 garlic cloves, crushed

1 teaspoon ground cumin

½ teaspoon ground allspice

½ teaspoon cayenne pepper

2 x 400 g cans diced tomatoes

1 cup (250 ml) fish or chicken stock

2 bay leaves

2 teaspoons thyme leaves

100 g okra, halved lengthways (optional)

500 g green prawns, peeled and deveined

150 g scallop meat

500 g firm white fish fillets, such as ling

Heat the oil in a large saucepan and add the onion and capsicum. Cook over medium heat for a few minutes, until soft. Add the garlic and spices and cook for 1 minute, stirring. Add the tomatoes, stock, bay leaves, thyme and okra, and simmer, uncovered, for 10 minutes.

Add the seafood to the pan and bring back to the boil. Reduce the heat so the mixture is just simmering and cook for about 5 minutes, stirring occasionally, until the seafood is cooked. Serve with rice.

SERVES 4-6

Birthday girl

When you and your wife have been together for a long time and her birthday comes along, what do you do? Push the panic button and go into stress mode? I reckon just about every bloke out there can relate to that. Men will surely understand the feeling that it's virtually impossible to buy a suitable present. Everything you think of, she already has! Desperation creeps in. And then despair. You feel that you are wasting your time in some ways, because you've got absolutely no idea what to do. Well, I have the answer!

It was Kell's thirtieth birthday and she was in the last two weeks of her pregnancy with Josh. I thought of going out somewhere … anywhere! But that was a little bit daunting: what if the baby decided to make an appearance earlier than anticipated! A trip away was out of the question for the same reason, so I put my thinking cap on. 'Eureka!' I thought. 'Rather than Mohammad going to the mountain, the mountain can come to Mohammad!'

My plan was simple but perfect: I organised for caterers from the James Street Cooking School to come to our home and prepare a private dinner for two! How great was that? The solution to every male's birthday problems.

It was a fantastic experience because we were in the comfort of our own home and the food was superb. The chef cooked the most incredible scallop dish and also a steak dish. And, of course, we had access to our very own cellar. It was wonderful. Even though we eat out often, it was one of our top nights of all time. First class.

What better birthday present? And a really special night.

Scallops with coconut rice

juice of 1 lime

1 tablespoon olive oil

1 red chilli, finely chopped

1 garlic clove, finely chopped

½ teaspoon grated fresh ginger

1 teaspoon ground cumin

pinch each of sugar, salt and freshly ground black pepper

1 cup (200 g) long grain white rice (jasmine is good)

1¼ cups (300 ml) coconut milk, approximately

36 scallops

12 cleaned double scallop shells

extra lime juice, to serve

coriander leaves, to garnish

Preheat a BBQ plate. Combine the lime juice, olive oil, chilli, garlic, ginger, cumin and seasonings in a small food processor or mortar and pestle and blend until smooth.

To make the coconut rice, place the rice and 1 cup (250 ml) of the coconut milk into a large saucepan. Add 1 cup (250 ml) of cold water (or fish or vegie stock if you like), cover and bring to the boil. Reduce the heat to low and cook for 6 minutes, then turn off the heat and stand, covered, for 10 minutes.

Place three scallops into each shell. Place a teaspoon of the spice mixture onto the scallops, along with a teaspoon of coconut milk. Put the shells onto the BBQ plate. Once the liquid starts to bubble inside the shells, time them to cook for about 30 seconds. The scallops will be white when cooked, but take care not to overcook them.

Serve with the coconut rice, an extra squeeze of lime juice and garnish with coriander.

SERVES 4

The snapper king

Kell and I first met Andrew Mirosch when we were developing a love for Stradbroke Island and he was a chef there at the Whale's Way Restaurant. It was there that we began our friendship and, later, we became really good fishing mates. For the record, although he is a much better cook than I am, there is absolutely no question that I am the Snapper King.

Andrew is a now a columnist, a TV presenter and the executive chef at the Sirromet multi-award-winning restaurant Lurleen's, which is nestled in the hills of picturesque Mount Cotton, a fine region between Brisbane and the Gold Coast. Lurleen's is ranked one of Australia's best five winery restaurants by the food industry's peak national body (Restaurant & Catering Awards for excellence 2007). In 2008, it was voted 'Best Restaurant in Queensland' (*Courier-Mail* Lifestyle Awards).

Because of our busy lifestyles, we don't often get the chance to go fishing any more, but there has been a lot of jousting about it in the media. Hopefully, I'll have the last laugh in this little segment of the book!

Andrew's great strength in cooking is that he lets the produce shine without really hammering the flavours of the food by over-spicing. He has a good balance in his food, which is something I've learnt from him. Sometimes, less is better. If you have great-quality produce, you're very lucky – and fortune certainly smiles on Lurleen's. Much of the produce is grown there and the chefs have access to beautiful fresh fruit and vegetables. Nearby, the Redlands area, too, grows wonderful produce, like the mouth-watering strawberries and fantastic, fresh green vegetables. Andrew uses these in his cooking.

What better chef could I have chosen to prepare a surprise family celebration for Mum and Dad's fortieth wedding anniversary?

Crumbed snapper

One of the great things about life on Queensland's North Stradbroke Island is the people I meet. Take, for example, Andrew Mirosch, a renowned chef who now resides with his beautiful young family on Straddie. He is a champion bloke; a real character, too, with dreadlocks in his hair and built like an outhouse!

Andrew is such an uncomplicated person and I guess that's the reason we get on so well, even though we come from such different professions. When we are together he doesn't want to talk about cooking and I don't want to talk about cricket. But we share a love of fishing, much to our partners' frustrations. There have been times when we have 'conned' our lovely ladies into allowing us a day out on the boat – pushing all the limits of household harmony, we head out as early as we can and arrive home as late as we can!

On one occasion we planned to fish an area known as 'The Cathedrals' just outside Moreton Bay, but had to wait for the weather to break. This turned into a game of patience, but the wait was worth it: when Andrew and I got out there, we cleaned up! Andrew reckons I ate 3½ kilos of snapper by myself that day, which is probably on the money.

Snapper come from deep waters to breed in the shallow waters of North Straddie during June, July and August. Fishing for snapper is just the ultimate break!

With fishing, you have to be so dedicated – and I'm passionate about my fishing! I have a saying: 'If you miss the finer details, then you never unlock the key to a fishing spot.' By this I mean that if you don't put in the time, effort and preparation, you mostly come home disappointed. It is a big ocean; and while you have to have luck, people who have the knowledge generally catch the fish.

We caught six or seven really good eating snapper, much to the delight of my daughter, Grace, who was 15 months old at the time. One of these fish was only a couple of inches bigger than she was, and she danced around it saying, 'Ish! Ish!'

Our celebration of the fishing day came through as a magnificent meal of crumbed snapper that night.

Crumbed snapper

This is a perfect meal for the start of summer, served with a simple green salad with a zesty dressing.

4 snapper fillets, skin removed
½ cup (60 g) cornflour
salt and pepper
4 eggs
1 ½ cups (150 g) breadcrumbs
1 cup (250 ml) extra virgin olive oil
1 garlic clove, halved
sprig of rosemary
⅓ cup (80 ml) lemon juice
⅓ cup (80 ml) balsamic vinegar

Put the cornflour onto a plate and season with salt and pepper. Lightly beat the eggs in a shallow bowl, and put the breadcrumbs onto another plate. Dust the snapper fillets in cornflour, dip into the egg, then coat with breadcrumbs. Set aside on a plate.

Heat the oil, garlic and rosemary in a heavy-based frying pan until very hot. Cook the snapper fillets in two batches for about 2 minutes each side, until golden brown. Transfer to a plate lined with paper towels.

Drain out the oil and wipe the crumbs out of the pan with a paper towel. Return the garlic and rosemary to the pan. Add the balsamic vinegar and simmer for about 4 minutes, until reduced by a third. Add the lemon juice and season with salt and pepper to taste.

Serve the fish with the sauce on the side for drizzling.

SERVES 4

Chicken

The greatest sledge

I was playing at the SCG in one of the dead-rubber games of the 2005 VB one-day series. We had won the toss and batted first and I was opening with Gilly. I reckon I scored about 40 off 55 balls, which is fair going for an opening batsman, but I could see why the crowd was getting agitated. Gilly, at the other end, was red hot and it would have been like watching the highlights from one end only. 'Chalk and cheese' come to mind. I was batting solidly but not setting the world on fire. At the time, my position in the team was coming under question and the spectators were definitely on my case, to the point where I got booed off the ground by my home Aussie crowd.

Change of innings: the opposition got through the first 15 overs and I was out on the square-leg boundary, getting heckled big-time by this one bloke who was sitting high up in the Dougie Walters stand. He yelled, "Ey, 'ayden! Yer batting's ****!'

Well, everyone is entitled to his own opinion, I thought.

But he wasn't letting up. "Ey, 'ayden! Can ya 'ear me?'

I could hear him all right. Everyone in the SCG could!

'Ya should be outta the team. Give someone else a go! Give Katich a go, yer dill!' he bawled, as he downed another beer. I was totally ignoring him, giving him absolutely nothing, until finally he bellowed like a bull: 'And, 'ayden, by the way, yer chicken casserole tastes like ****!'

That was it! I just had to laugh. His persistence had paid off. I couldn't resist a reply and turned around, shouting back: 'Well, you bought it, you mug!' I added as politely as I could under the circumstances: 'Oh, and by the way, thanks for the 30 bucks. I'll have a beer on you tonight, you clown!'

The crowd loved it. So did I!

Kell's asparagus chicken casserole

There are times when the plane is coming in to land at Brisbane airport after an overseas or interstate tour that I swear I can smell Kell's asparagus chicken casserole cooking in the oven! This is my favourite dish made with love from my favourite girl. It was also the first-ever dish she made for me when we met.

Before I even met her, Kell always cooked it for her parents and two brothers. Kell learned to cook the dish at school in Year 10 during a Home Economics class, and over the years she has really perfected it. Because she knew it so well, she had the confidence to cook it for me during the early stages of our courting. It has been a winner ever since!

When we are touring Australia and Kell is travelling with me, it is an easy dish for her to make, a meal where everything gets thrown in.

Kell's asparagus chicken casserole is so popular. Good things are meant to be shared, especially with family, so her recipe has now gone 1500 kilometres up to North Queensland to my brother, Gary. He loves good food, too, so his insistence on having the recipe for Kell's dish speaks for itself.

Kell is a really good cook. Simple is best with her. And, more than anything, our love of food has been one of the key ingredients for our life in marriage. It is something we share and do well together. Just sitting around the kitchen in the evening, preparing a meal, is one of the highlights of our day.

When we travel, one thing we really love doing is experiencing eating in different places, be it in Venice or Brisbane. But having said that, there is nothing quite like a simple home-cooked meal and Kell does that fabulously, with her asparagus chicken casserole at the top of the list.

Kell's asparagus chicken casserole

Chicken thighs are more flavoursome than breast fillets, but are higher in fat. Serve this dish with steamed vegetables and steamed basmati rice, if you like.

½ cup (75 g) plain flour
salt and pepper
4 chicken breast or thigh fillets
1 tablespoon olive oil
1 teaspoon butter
1 onion, finely diced
2 garlic cloves, crushed
6 button mushrooms, thickly sliced
2 x 400 g cans cream of asparagus soup
juice of 1 lemon

Preheat the oven to 180°C.

Combine the flour, salt and pepper on a plate. Cut each of the fillets into three pieces. Dust the chicken with the seasoned flour, shaking off the excess.

Heat the oil and butter in a frying pan and add the onion and garlic. Cook until soft and brown, then remove from the pan leaving behind the oil and butter.

Add the chicken to the pan and cook until well browned.

Place the chicken into a large casserole dish along with the onion mixture and the mushrooms.

Pour the soup and lemon juice over the chicken. Cover and bake for 45 minutes.

SERVES 4

Crispy chicken

Crispy chicken has its origins in North Queensland – a location that is a favourite playground of mine with its national parks, Atherton Tableland lakes, beautiful islands, beaches and spectacular Great Barrier Reef. There's something really special about the north. My brother, Gary, lives there on the coast near Ingham, with his wife, Alex, and their children. We have spent hours marauding around the countryside, fishing, hunting pigs and riding horses – though Gary is no horseman!

Once Gary and I were riding along Forrest Beach when he came unstuck and ended up with a mouthful of sand. The horse had merely gone from a walk to a trot!

Concerned locals moved towards him, checking and inquiring about his wellbeing, to which Gary replied, 'I'm fine. Just breaking the horse in.' The truth of the matter was the horse was 15 years old and as timid as they come!

That coastal region, about 100 kilometres north of Townsville, is a glorious place where a cooling wind blows continuously off the ocean. No better climate exists in their so-called 'winter' months! It's a great place for just getting back to nature. Gary reckons that when I get up there, put on my weather-worn old hat and go unshaven, I look like Jungle Jim.

Gary and Alex used to live in a shack right on the beach at a place called Cassidy Beach. Recently, a woman was walking along that beach and thought she spied a log ahead in the sand – only to see it grow legs and scurry into the water! Another woman was driving at night towards a nearby town called Lucinda when she saw a 2-metre crocodile on the road ahead. Locals in this region have learned to just live with crocs.

It was at the Cassidy Beach shack that Alex relayed messages to Gary regarding my first-ever Test century against the West Indies. Gary was windsurfing, too nervous to watch the television, and asked his wife to use different coloured towels to signal my progress towards the 100.

The shack had great atmosphere. Its location and views, too, were spectacular. You had the impression, though, that great damage could be done to it, especially by winds associated with North Queensland's cyclonic weather! A recent cyclone was the reason Gary, Alex and their three children moved to a safer location.

Crispy chicken is actually a dish that Alex once cooked for us and, like many dishes, has been tasted, enjoyed and prepared again and again. That Alex was able to weave her magic in the shack's very limited kitchen and conjure up quality meals, like crispy chicken, remains a credit to her.

When I first went up there to visit, Alex used to feed me what Gary ate. She is a great cook but Gary loves his creamy dishes and pasta and, especially when I'm in training, I need to watch my diet. Kell keeps me on track with this when I am at home. I can hear her saying in answer to questions about food, 'We have learned that we have to watch what Matt eats because he is in training.'

The pasta and creamy dishes are gone from the menu when I am in town, but crispy chicken has stood the test of time.

Crispy chicken

This chicken is beautiful served with roast vegies in winter, or a salad in summer.

2 cups (500 ml) soy sauce
¾ cup (185 ml) sherry
3 cups (750 ml) water
1 onion, finely chopped
1 tablespoon chopped fresh ginger
½ cup (100 g) brown sugar
1 whole chicken (no. 18)

Put the soy sauce, sherry, water, onion, ginger and sugar into a very large pot. Stir over medium heat to dissolve the sugar, then bring to the boil. Turn the heat down to low. Tuck the chicken wings under the body and put the chicken into the liquid, breast side down.

Simmer gently for 30 minutes. Preheat the oven to 180°C.

Carefully lift the chicken from the pan and place breast side up on a wire rack in a baking pan. Cook in the oven for 30 minutes, until the skin is crisp.

SERVES 4

Hallowed ground

My son Joshua's first experience of a Test match was in London, at Lord's, the home of cricket. Any opportunity a cricketer gets to play on that hallowed turf is to be grasped in both hands and regarded as the highlight of his career.

I can remember driving down from Manchester in 1991 just to see Lord's. Middlesex were playing a home game but there weren't many people there so it was possible to get a feel for the ground, for the Marylebone Cricket Club and for the training facilities. I could tell that despite being a cricketer, as a walk-up punter there was absolutely no way I would be able to go anywhere close to the ground. Even the thought of setting a foot on it would be enough for the 'wallopers' with their big black caps on to come round and push me into the back of the divvy van!

Lord's is a cricket oval patronised by power 'players', be they political, social or religious. It's the meeting place of a hotchpotch of socialites and iconic figures. I recall a Test match I played there before the 2005 Ashes and Queen Elizabeth II shook our hands. Our then prime minister, John Howard, has made the trek there, too. Prime ministers from all around the globe attended the first Test of the 2005 Ashes. But what made it so special for me was that Joshy, Grace and Kell came, as well as our friends Seb and Bart Wilson. Well, at the end of the Test, they were all in the change room to celebrate our first win against England, who we absolutely hammered.

We really rubbed it into the Poms, too. Strains of the Aussie team's song could be heard coming from the change room. We marched across the gallows, as it were, into enemy territory and really drove it into them! England had not won a Lord's Test match for a long time and, in that moment, we were the victors and we sung and celebrated into the night. Maybe the gods of cricket looked down and snarled at us, because it was the last game we won during that Ashes tour.

Previously, in 2001, we had been encouraged to get out of the ground as soon as the match had ended. I remember writing in my newspaper article at the time that even a seagull was chased off the bloody ground! But in 2005, I had my children, especially Grace, as Josh was still a baby, playing around with Harry Gilchrist and Holly and James McGrath. There they were, running on the wicket, running on the covers, playing on all the tractors. The background was the Lord's pavilion, and we had won the Test, so it was a privileged moment to have my children out on the ground with all the other members of our family. Just unbelievable!

A picture tells a thousand words. Josh will never remember that significant Test match but Kelly, Grace and I will, and, I guess, that's how memories live on. There will be photos to say he was there. He will be proud and, even if he grows up to hate cricket, he will still understand one day, when he has the wonderful opportunity to travel overseas, just how lucky he was to be able to run around the ground, to look through the Long Room and the Lord's change room, to stand on the balcony and hear the ovation for the Australian team.

Yes, there is something almost bordering on the sacred about Lord's .

Macadamia and feta stuffed chicken

When Kell was pregnant with Grace, her favourite meal was macadamia and feta stuffed chicken (though at the time, I made it without feta). Just as Kell loves making her asparagus chicken because she knows it's a favourite of mine, I love cooking her her favourite meal, too. Kell was off her food during her pregnancy and, in desperation, I made this dish for her one night. She loved it!

As blokes, I guess we just don't understand the hardship endured by women during pregnancy – there are some smells and tastes which could not be less enticing. So I kept it simple. I stuffed the meat with English spinach, toasted pinenuts and herbs – not too hard on the old tummy – and avoided garlic and feta, both no-no's during Kell's pregnancy.

While the dish started out simple enough – not too rich – after little Gracey was born and we were relaxing back on Stradbroke Island, the recipe evolved and I started getting more adventurous with the stuffing.

It's always fascinating to hear pregnancy tales, especially those related to food and cravings – the different experiences that make individual pregnancies so unique. Good food and milk were always on the menu with Kell's pregnancy and this dish is now one of Grace's favourites, too. Pregnancy and childbirth are truly a miracle. Fatherhood is a blessing!

Macadamia and feta stuffed chicken

You could use marinated feta in this recipe to create a slightly different flavour. A 350 g jar of marinated feta will give you about 200 g of feta after draining.

⅓ cup (50 g) sesame seeds
2 tablespoons olive oil
1 onion, finely chopped
2 bacon rashers, finely chopped
3 garlic cloves, crushed
200 g feta, chopped
⅓ cup (50 g) macadamias, very finely chopped
2 teaspoons chopped fresh thyme
2 teaspoons chopped fresh rosemary
salt and pepper
4 chicken breast fillets

Preheat the oven to 180°C. Place the sesame seeds into a dry frying pan and cook over medium heat, stirring occasionally, for 5 minutes, until golden brown. Transfer to a plate to cool.

Heat half the olive oil in a frying pan and cook the onion, bacon and garlic until lightly browned. Transfer to a large bowl, and cool.

Add the feta, macadamias, sesame seeds and herbs to the onion mixture, and season to taste. Mix with your hands to form a paste.

Cut each chicken fillet in half lengthways horizontally, to make long flat steaks.

Divide the mixture between each piece of chicken, placing it in the centre. Roll the chicken around the stuffing and secure with a toothpick.

Place on an oven tray, brush with remaining olive oil and bake for 25 minutes, until cooked through.

SERVES 4

Nola's chicken pie

It's funny the direction life takes you when you follow your instincts.

The first time I came off the Gabba – back in 1991, my debut – I had made 149 against South Australia and there was this little fella yelling out, 'Matty! Matty! Matty!' I knew I couldn't speak to him then, but as I walked into the dressing room I can remember thinking, 'I reckon I'll go back and have a bit of a chat with that little shaver. He looked a really decent kid!'

After having a shower, I brought my gear up to air it in the sun and then went over to this little bloke and asked him his name.

He was Bart, 10 years old, and he looked me excitedly in the eyes and asked, 'Please sign my bat?'

As a young 'un, good manners were really stressed by my parents and, without hesitation, I said to him, 'With pleasure.' I asked him where he was from and he told me Coolum, on the Sunshine Coast of Queensland.

He went on, 'I hear you love surfing, Mr Hayden. Why don't you drive up and come for a surf with me and my family?'

His parents, Nola and Mick Wilson, heard this and laughed, but something instinctively told me they were really good people and I would certainly be very welcome. Bart, handing me a pencil and paper, said, 'Here's our address.'

With laughter in the background, I took down Bart's address.

A few weeks later, I headed to the Sunshine Coast and, again instinctively, decided to look them up. To this day they are some of my best friends. Bart was page boy at our wedding.

Young Bart has grown up now, along with his brothers, Julian and Seb. Julian is one of the best surfers in the world, contracted by a major surfing company. And Seb and Bart are Australian long-board champions and compete internationally.

They have this house at Coolum and when you walk into it you get an amazing feeling. You sense the walls would not be standing but for the blue tac and glue holding the photos on. There are pics of the boys growing up, surfing, and some with me and my girls. It's really wonderful!

Nola said Bart always gravitated towards me. There was a real connection. One day, when he was young, he had written me a birthday card and was hoping to see me at the Gabba to give it to me. After batting, I must have stayed under the grandstand and, apparently, he was so disappointed that he cried. Nola then told him to put the card under the windscreen of my car. I'll never forget that birthday card. It was really appreciated.

Meeting the Wilsons taught me a lesson that if you open your eyes to people it's amazing who you can meet. As a sportsman, I'm privileged to travel all around the world, but it doesn't take much to give someone a moment of your time. I did that with Bart and, for me, it opened up a wonderfully generous family.

Her kindness aside, Nola's other great attribute is her chicken pie. Believe me, after spending hours in the surf, all you want to do is eat, and Nola makes this massive chicken pie that feeds the five of us – and after surfing, I am usually as hungry as ten men! It is an old-fashioned classic that fits the bill perfectly after rolling around in the surf and the sand for hours on end.

Nola's chicken pie

1 whole BBQ chicken
1 tablespoon butter
1 onion, chopped
100 g button mushrooms, halved and sliced
1 tablespoon plain flour
½ cup (125 ml) milk
½ cup (125 ml) chicken stock
1 cup (150 g) frozen peas, thawed
2 hard-boiled eggs, quartered
375 g block frozen puff pastry, thawed
milk, to brush

Preheat the oven to 190°C.

Pull the meat from the chicken and tear into bite-sized pieces; set aside. Melt the butter in a frying pan and cook the onion until soft. Add the mushrooms and cook until they are just soft.

Sprinkle the flour over the onion mixture and cook, stirring, for about 30 seconds.

Gradually add the combined milk and stock, stirring constantly. Bring to the boil, then reduce the heat and simmer for 3 minutes.

Stir the chicken and the peas into the sauce. Spoon into a 4-cup capacity pie dish (with a lip) and arrange the egg quarters into the mixture.

Roll out the pastry so that it is about 3 cm bigger than the pie dish. Cut long strips (about 1 cm wide) from the pastry and press onto the lip of the dish. Wipe a little water onto the pastry strips with your fingers.

Lay the remaining pastry over the dish. Trim the overhanging pastry with a small sharp knife, and press the edges with a fork to seal. Brush lightly with milk, and prick some holes in the top. Bake for 30 minutes, until the pastry is golden brown.

SERVES 6

Chicken curry

It goes without saying that on a cricket tour to the subcontinent, when I walk into a kitchen to watch a chef make a meal, it blows the staff's minds away! The kitchenhands are infatuated, and incredibly surprised, that a cricketer, let alone a well-known cricketer, is sharing their workspace with them. It just shocks them! When I walk into their kitchen there is a hush. The chef and assistants all try to get on with their business, and they are very attentive to their jobs, but I can feel my presence is creating great interest. There is the odd whisper and an occasional voice can be heard.

Sri Lanka is the more laidback part of the subcontinent. There is much less hustle and bustle than in India. Like Indians, Sri Lankans are not loud-speaking. Their voices do not boom out and dominate the streets. But in India, it is considered good luck to touch the fortunate, so the Indians are much more tactile than Sri Lankans.

There is no problem with your safety. Indians are not aggressive, but when they see you, you feel like The Beatles must have felt. It is like Beatlemania! For a country boy, it blows me away that I have that type of impact on people. By contrast, the Sri Lankans tend to look from afar. And so they did this evening in the hotel we were staying at, when I enjoyed the enlightening experience of learning the subtle touches of making a curry from a local chef.

Curry on the subcontinent is considered a status symbol. If a potential wife can make a curry, it is considered such a gift that it can be included in a bride's dowry.

I said to this chef from the hotel, 'If I learn nothing else tonight, I don't mind. Just as long as I'm taught how to make a good fluffy rice, I'll be more than happy.' What a joy it was for me to mix with those people, become one with them and learn from them.

Because rice is the staple diet of billions of people, it is a critical part of life in any home in the region. Like we have bread, they have rice. Like we have sandwiches, they have soft, fluffy rice that can come fried or sweetened with fruits in it. A typical rice meal might be served with two curries, a form of bread and a kind of coconut sambal, a spicy sauce and some chutneys. It is a busy meal that you eat with your hands.

But rice is the foundation of any meal, and it was a joy to stand at the coalface with these delightful, polite Sri Lankan chefs and kitchen staff and learn the way to cook the dish that is responsible for keeping billions of people satisfied with food in their stomachs.

Chicken curry

2 tablespoons ground coriander

2 teaspoons sweet paprika

2 teaspoons curry powder

2 teaspoons salt

1 teaspoon chilli powder

½ teaspoon ground turmeric

pinch ground cloves

pinch ground cardamom

6 chicken thigh cutlets

3 teaspoons vegetable oil

1 onion, finely chopped

3 garlic cloves, crushed

1 teaspoon grated fresh ginger

3 curry leaves or bay leaves

1 stalk lemon grass, white part only

2 green chillies, deseeded and finely chopped

2 tomatoes, diced

2 cinnamon sticks

1 cup (250 ml) coconut milk

½ cup (125 ml) water

steamed basmati rice, to serve

Combine the coriander, paprika, curry powder, salt, chilli powder, turmeric, cloves and cardamom. Rub all over the chicken, cover the chicken with plastic wrap and refrigerate for 4 hours.

Heat the oil in a large saucepan and cook the onion until soft and brown. Add the garlic, ginger, curry leaves, lemon grass, chilli, tomato and cinnamon sticks and cook over low heat for 3 minutes, stirring regularly.

Add the chicken, cover and cook over medium heat for 5 minutes. Add the coconut milk and water, bring slowly to boil and simmer for 20 minutes. Take out the cinnamon sticks, lemon grass and bay leaves before serving.

Serve with rice.

SERVES 4-6

Chicken tikka

500 g chicken thigh fillets
2 tablespoons thick plain yoghurt
1 tablespoon garlic paste
1 tablespoon ginger paste
2 teaspoons red chilli powder
2 teaspoons ground cumin
1 teaspoon garam masala
2 teaspoons lemon juice
good pinch of salt

Trim excess fat from the chicken, and cut into 3 cm cubes. Place into a ceramic or glass dish.

Combine the remaining ingredients, add to the chicken and turn to coat well. Cover with plastic wrap and refrigerate for at least 2 hours, or overnight.

Soak eight 20 cm bamboo skewers in water for 20 minutes. Heat a BBQ or chargrill until moderately hot. Thread the chicken onto the skewers. Cook for 12 minutes, turning occasionally to cook evenly.

SERVES 4

Meat

Gabby's lasagne

Gracie's favourite meal, Gabby's lasagne, has its roots in a magnificent Italian district that is renowned as the culinary capital of Italy. The town of Ortona, in the Abruzzo district of Italy, is a gloriously beautiful mountainside village wedged up against the seaside. Such is its culinary reputation that Italy's most promising chefs are sent to the town to ply their craft.

Gabby, the mother of our beautiful deceased friend, Daniela, was raised in the Ortona township which, although flattened during World War II, remains overflowing with history.

Now Gabby resides in Brisbane, having followed her husband (coincidentally named Gabriele) from Italy to Queensland in 1965.

They are typically hard-working Italians. Gabriele was a cane cutter at Finch Hatton, west of Mackay, which is a settlement in the Pioneer Valley that leads to the lovely rainforests of Eungella, about 80 kilometres west of the Coral Coast. For six months of the year he would cut cane, and for the other six months he would join Gabby working at the cannery in Brisbane.

Gabby, now a renowned dressmaker, is a person who would do anything for anybody. Her son-in-law, Kevin, who was married to Daniela, affectionately refers to her as Alice, the character from *The Brady Bunch*, because she will arrive for a visit but end up doing the cleaning and the cooking. If you go away on holidays, she will mow the lawn. She treats Kevin's dogs, Roxy and Heidi, like they are her grandchildren.

Our daughter, Grace, just loves Gabby. She goes to the same church as we do, and Gracie will spend the entire service walking between her mother and Gabby.

Grace gives Gabby great joy and this warms our hearts like we never could have imagined. People ask what is Grace's favourite age for us. 'Every day!' I reply. Why? She makes me laugh so much all the time. She's a real little mimic with her individual sense of humour. Gracie and I have an amazing bond. It doesn't matter whether I've been away for three months or two weeks, when we're back together we're able to pick up where we left off.

She is a wonderful child who has brought great joy to Kell's parents who had to deal with the tragedy of losing their son, Chris, when he was 19.

Gracie calls Kell's mum Mama, and Kell's dad Cookie, because he loves eating cookies with his cup of tea.

I'm sure she also calls Gabby, in her mind at least, the best cook around. Gabby's lasagne is a beauty which Gracie mops up, then comes back for seconds. Our entire family is blessed for the role Gabby plays in all of our lives.

Gabby's lasagne

Good on the night but not bad either after having a 'sleep' in the fridge!

2 tablespoons olive oil

1 onion, finely chopped

2 garlic cloves, crushed

500 g lean beef mince

¼ cup (60 ml) white wine

400 g can peeled whole Roma tomatoes

700 g bottle of Italian tomato sauce (sugo)

2 teaspoons dried Italian herbs

beef or pork bone

large sprig fresh basil, chopped

2 x 250 g boxes instant lasagne sheets

1 teaspoon salt

1 teaspoon olive oil

100 g finely grated Parmesan cheese

100 g grated mild cheese (such as tasty)

100 g grated mozzarella cheese

Heat the oil in a large saucepan and cook the onion and garlic until soft and lightly brown. Add the mince, breaking it up with a wooden spoon, and cook until all the liquid has evaporated. Add the white wine and cook until evaporated, then add the tomatoes, tomato sauce and herbs.

Add the meat bone and simmer over low heat, partially covered, for 1 hour. Add the basil 15 minutes before the sauce is cooked.

Meanwhile, bring a large pot of water to the boil, add salt and olive oil. Add 4 lasagna sheets, one at a time, and cook for 5 minutes until soft (move with a fork to help keep the sheets separate). Lift out with a large slotted spoon into cold water to stop the cooking process, then drain on a clean cotton table cloth or tea towels. Repeat with remaining lasagne sheets. Preheat the oven to 180°C.

To assemble the lasagne, layer the pasta sheets, meat sauce and combined cheeses in a large (10-cup capacity) lasagne dish. Tuck the top layer of pasta sheets in at the sides, and finish with a thin layer of meat sauce then a topping of the combined cheeses.

Bake for 30 minutes, until the cheese is lightly browned.

SERVES 8

Grandma's shepherd's pie

My life growing up in the country is full of rich, wonderful memories that time shall never diminish. One such memory is enjoying the love and attention of my grandparents in Kingaroy, and the wondrous cooking of my beloved Grandma.

After my dad purchased our property from Grandma and Pop, they relocated to live in a fairly central part of Kingaroy, within close walking distance to school and church. Every Sunday we would all go to Mass and then on to Grandma and Pop's place where a Sunday roast was a tradition.

Sunday lunch was very much a part of Australian bush culture. It was the one time in the week when a family was able to sit down and spend quality time together. After lunch, too, was special. Visitors and relatives would drop in and either chat with Mum and Grandma or play billiards with Pop and Dad. The kids would play cricket with one of the next-door neighbours or, when we were tall enough to put our noses over the billiard table and hold a cue, join in with Pop and Dad. Everyone would eagerly await afternoon tea, and Grandma's malted milks are still rave material!

During the week Dad would be out working on the property and Mum, a teacher, would be at school, sometimes working after school helping students, going to staff meetings or doing extracurricular activities like producing and directing school musicals.

Our very early cricket years were spent playing Junior Cricket. This was mainly played on Saturday mornings, so Sunday was a grand gathering.

I remember Grandma always had leftovers from the Sunday roast dinner, that were ground up in an old-style hand mincer. It didn't matter what type of roast meat was left over – pork, lamb, beef. It was a very, very simple way to make the roast extend for another two lunches during the week – or even for smoko for the farmhands, in earlier times. Grandma would put the minced-up meat into a baking dish, put mashed potato on top and bake it until it was a golden brown on top. It was a great feed!

I had a great relationship with my grandparents. One of the greatest things you can do is enjoy the love of grandparents. I was very fortunate with my grandparents, on both sides of our family. It is so important and such a beautiful part of a child's development because, I believe, while it is a parent's job to discipline children, it is a grandparent's job to spoil them with love.

So much wisdom comes from older people, who are often ready and willing to invest time in people's lives, and kids are 'sponges' for that. Grandma and Pop spoiled my brother, Gary, and myself. Pop would tell me intriguing stories about the land, and every afternoon I would go to his house, which was only seconds from the school, to wait for Mum to finish work. Some days I would even go there for lunch and that was always a treat.

Grandma would spoil us rotten! I didn't have Vegemite sandwiches for lunch. It would be a three-course meal!

Grandma and Pop grew everything in their garden – lettuce, carrots, beans, peas, potatoes – vegetables of all kinds! Peach trees, in season, had their branches fully burdened with huge, juicy, delicious fruit and their grapes tasted just so good. Chutney was made from tomatoes and various home-grown fruits, and Grandma's jams, made from figs, strawberries, gooseberries, mulberries, oranges, or any other fruit that was in season, were always a treat, especially on hot scones or pikelets.

The chookhouse, too, had its place! Fresh eggs were always added to other ingredients and whisked up into some magical culinary delights. Many a chook ate up well, only to be beheaded, plucked and cleaned and then cooked and eaten heartily!

They were different days and it is sad as they are kind of 'lost' days.

It meant so much to me as a kid to have grandparents in my life. I believe that through their love, care, kindness and the traditions they passed on, I have been given great gifts and am determined never to lose them. It was a wonderful thing, knowing how much my grandparents loved me and how much, in return, they also were loved.

So that's why I have put Grandma's shepherd's pie in this book. It is part of my tradition, my memories, and I want to keep them always.

Grandma's shepherd's pie

Shepherd's pie is traditionally made from lamb, but you could also use leftover roast beef.

600 g cooked roast lamb
1 cup (250 ml) beef stock
2 teaspoons cornflour or arrowroot
salt and pepper
2 teaspoons olive oil
2 onions, halved and finely sliced
4 tomatoes, finely sliced
1 kg potatoes, peeled and chopped
¼ cup (60 ml) milk
2 tablespoons butter

Preheat the oven to 180°C.

Mince the meat in a food processor, or an old-fashioned hand-operated mincer if you have one. Place into an 8-cup capacity baking dish.
Mix the beef stock with the cornflour, and season with salt and pepper. Pour over the mince.

Heat the oil in a frying pan and cook the onions until soft and lightly browned. Layer the onions and tomatoes over the mince.

Meanwhile, boil the potatoes until tender. Drain well then mash with the milk, butter and a pinch of salt. Spoon the mash over the top of the filling to form a thick crust. Bake for about 45 minutes, until golden brown.

SERVES 6

Kerry Packer

He has been called a smart entrepreneur, a risk-taker, a national larrikin, a spontaneous philanthropist, the most successful businessman of his generation. In the 1970s, he not only created World Series Cricket but also changed the game's image forever. He revolutionised television coverage of cricket (indeed, of sport in general) and even the way the game was played.

So when Alan Jones, a friend of Kerry Packer's, dined with Kell and me at our home, the dinner conversation soon turned to the one-day game and the inspirational figure behind World Series Cricket.

'Mate, I'd absolutely love to meet Kerry Packer,' I said.

Next thing I know, Alan has organised for me to meet the great man. I was absolutely honoured. I invited my old friends Steve Waugh (Tugger) and Justin Langer (Alfie) and a couple of the younger fellas, Brett Lee (Binga) and Shane Watson (Watto), to join me.

Now, the Aussie team is divided into Nerds (traditional, conservative dressers) and Julios (slick, modern ones). Dressing sharp, streaking hair and using gel is left to the Julios, and for the rest of us Nerds, what to wear isn't usually part of the conversation. When we asked what we should wear for this occasion, we were told 'something casual and comfortable'. Binga and Watto, members of the young brigade and fully fledged Julios, did exactly that. Tugger (ex-Nerd) wore a suit and tie and, despite what was said, Alfie and I wore our Aussie suits and ties. 'Nerds' — and proud of the name! We were meeting a legend. This was an event.

As we waited to meet Kerry, the atmosphere was electric. We also felt a little nervous, not because it was the night before the Super Series Test, but because we were meeting a very skilled tactician. Kerry Packer would have an opportunity to put us all in the 'cricket' hot seat!

Once we'd arrived at his home and had all been introduced to the great man, Alan and Kerry engaged in some enjoyable verbal jousting. Then Kerry turned to Tugger, who'd just finished writing his autobiography, and said, 'Son, who's opening your book launch?'

'The Prime Minister, Mr Packer.'

Kerry looked over at Alan and said, 'Well, Mr President, that's put you in your place!'

Before long, the conversation turned to cricket. Alfie was on the mat. 'Son,' said Kerry, 'explain to me why you get hit on the helmet so much.'

Poor old Alfie! He was quietly taken aback and mumbled 'I … er … don't really know.'

'Son,' responded Kerry, intent on getting straight to the point. 'You just can't be watching the ball.'

We looked apprehensively at each other. Tugger smirked. One down: three to go!

Kerry's belief in good luck, nurtured by his incredible gambling feats, was known to all of us, and it featured in the conversation. We were talking about Tony Greig's development of helmets. It was a significant part of the discourse and Kerry would not let it go. Just when Alfie thought he could relax, Kerry, with a twinkle in his eye, turned to him again. 'And, son, you should know all about luck. If Greig hadn't invented helmets, you'd be ******* dead!'

The rest of us were left unscathed. We had all dined out on Alfie!

The whole experience was a cracker. That one short meeting left a lasting impression on me. Kerry Packer was a great Australian who flew the Aussie flag high. He was a straight-shooter, an incredibly knowledgeable man and a wonderful communicator. He had a passion for the subjects about which he spoke, and you couldn't help but be drawn in. His opinions were strong and confronting. But we were proud of our achievements and Kerry was a great example of what could be done through hard work, determination and sheer Aussie grit.

Sadly, he died on Boxing Day in 2005. As the Australian team donned black armbands for the second day of the Test against South Africa, to pay tribute to Kerry Packer, I could hear Kerry's last words to me: 'Son, thank you so much for taking the time to come and meet me.' I knew in my heart that I would go on to make a century in that match.

Kerry Packer was a true blue, fair dinkum Aussie icon – a man among men.

KP Meat pie

⅓ cup (50 g) plain flour

salt and freshly ground black pepper

500 g blade or chuck steak, cut into 3 cm cubes

2 tablespoons olive oil

3 bacon rashers, chopped

2 onions, chopped

3 garlic cloves, finely chopped

2 cups (500 ml) beef or vegetable stock

2 sprigs rosemary

½ cup (125 ml) red wine

4 sheets frozen puff pastry, thawed

Put the flour into a plastic bag, season the flour with salt and pepper and add the meat. Twist the opening to seal, and shake to coat. Take the pieces out and shake off the excess. Heat half the oil in a large pan and cook the meat in 2 batches over moderately high heat until brown. Set aside.

Add the remaining oil, and cook the bacon until browned; set aside. Cook the onions and garlic over medium heat until soft and lightly browned. Return the steak and bacon to the pan, then add the stock gradually, stirring and scraping the bottom of the pan.

Add the rosemary and wine, cover and bring just to the boil. Turn the heat down to low and simmer for 1½ hours. Uncover and cook a further 30 minutes, until the meat is very tender. Cool completely before assembling the pie. This mixture could be made a day in advance, and the pie made the next day.

Preheat the oven to 200°C. Line a 23 cm, 4-cup capacity pie dish with a sheet of pastry. It won't cover the dish completely so make sure 2 sides are covered, then cut 2 wide strips from another sheet to cover the rest. Make sure you overlap the pastry well and press the joins together. Fill with the meat mixture.

Cut the remaining pastry into strips, and use to top the pie in a lattice pattern. Alternatively, just top with a sheet of pastry and cut some slits in the top for the steam to escape.

Bake for 10 minutes, then reduce the heat to 180°C and cook a further 50–60 minutes, until golden brown.

SERVES 6

Rissoles

These are easy to make and very versatile. You can eat them hot, with spaghetti and a tomato pasta sauce, or cold between a couple of slabs of fresh bread.

2 bread slices, crusts removed
1 kg beef mince
1 onion, finely chopped
2 garlic cloves, crushed
1 carrot, grated
2 eggs, lightly beaten
¼ cup (60 ml) BBQ sauce
½ teaspoon each of salt and pepper
1 cup (150 g) plain flour
2 tablespoons olive oil

Place the bread into a food processor and process briefly to make fresh breadcrumbs. Place the crumbs, mince, onion, garlic, carrot, eggs, BBQ sauce and salt and pepper into a bowl and use your hands to mix well.

Roll heaped tablespoons of the mixture into balls. Put the flour into a plastic bag, then add the meatballs and jiggle around to coat in the flour. Shake off excess flour.

Heat the oil in a large, heavy based frying pan. Cook in 2 batches over medium heat for 10 minutes, until well browned and cooked through. Return the first batch to the pan to warm through.

MAKES ABOUT 40

Traditional spaghetti sauce

I love my family and, in particular, the memories of sitting around sharing great food, wine, jokes and stories. This is part of my tradition. Life just wouldn't be the same without family. Fortunately, I have been privileged to be part of an exclusive, extended family, too – the Australian cricket team family. One that travels, trains, plays and eats together! A family with members who live in each other's pockets for ten-and-a-half months a year.

Talking about eating, one Aussie family member springs immediately to mind. Yes! None other than Merv Hughes whose popular joke is 'I'm on a diet! A seafood diet! I see food – and I eat it!' With such simple criteria in mind, cooking a meal for Merv is always a breeze!

It was in the summer of 1996, perhaps '95, and Queensland played Victoria at the Gabba. Queensland was in mucho trouble by the end of the third day. Dean 'Deano' Jones declared overnight and left us chasing a 300-plus total on the last day.

I had previously organised to host Merv at my home on that particular night. Well, by late afternoon, Merv was on fire! Victoria was on top and Merv just loved rubbing salt into our wounds. In the first innings, I was out for a duck – the big zero – and Merv just couldn't help himself! After the close of play that day, he sneaked into the Queensland dressing room and drew ducks over all my gear, especially my bat, as that was to be my tool of the trade the next morning.

Mum and Dad had travelled down from Kingaroy to watch the match at the Gabba and at the close of play I dashed up to the stands to let my parents know that Merv would be joining us for dinner at home in a short time. I had just phoned Kell and asked her to come as well.

Mum went into panic mode! 'Kell's fine! She's always a joy to have and easy to feed, but Merv?' she questioned. 'Matt, you're going to need a horse and cow to feed him!'

After me telling Mum not to worry and assuring her there was enough food in the house to appease Merv's incredible appetite, Mum turned to Dad and said, 'Well, thank heavens we brought down those three buckets of Grandma's peaches.'

Merv arrived for dinner as chirpy as a bird, very cocky and unbelievably jovial. We all set about creating the 'perfect meal'. I was particularly focused on the fact Merv had to bowl to me early the next morning!

'What have you got here, Haydos? Ah … peaches!' he exclaimed, and he devoured first one bucketful of peaches and then a second.

Now it's important for you to realise that Merv is one of the biggest con artists in the world. His ability to talk someone into doing anything is renowned. I realised he had Mum in mind as his next victim!

'OK, Haydos,' he said as he opened the kitchen cupboards. 'Now, what have we got here? Yep, this'll do, and this, and this, and ...' He continued until most of the food was taken from all the cupboards! I joined in, too, till the cupboards were bare.

'We need a really big saucepan. Yep,' he said, satisfied he had found the largest one in the kitchen, as he dipped in to take more peaches from a third bucket. 'Mmmmmmm, these peaches are really delicious!'

Anything and everything was thrown into the saucepan. Then Mum was called into the action while Kell and Dad looked on with interest and perhaps a slight sense of suspicion.

'You'll boil the kettle for me, won't you?' Merv asked Mum sweetly. Mum, at least, knew how to do that! We often tease Mum about her cooking and Merv knew that.

Now, Mum swears this next part of the story didn't happen, but Kell, Dad, Merv and I know it definitely did. Probably the whole of Australia knows now, as Merv uses this story as part of his repartee! He handed Mum a massive fist of spaghetti and asked her to put it into the kettle to cook. Mum was about to do that. Laughing, we all stopped her.

She always denies that story vehemently. 'I wouldn't have done that!' Then quickly concedes, 'Well, if it did happen it's probably because Merv is such a big con artist and, anyway,' she goes on, 'I would have thought, in the nicest possible way mind you, that Merv is a real character and he probably does boil spaghetti in his kettle!'

Kell's side of the story is that Mum did it all right, but she knew Merv was playing a trick and just went along with it to be a good sport.

Anyhow, it was a great meal. And the outcome had the desired effect.

Big Merv had to bowl to me first thing the next day. I'll never forget watching Merv as he came in bowling to me the next morning, with his big guts wobbling up and down full of Grandma's peaches and the huge meal he had devoured the previous night.

I believe I have never batted better than that day. The perfect meal produced perfect batting for me. My score was something like 200-plus not out and Queensland won the game just after tea.

Yes! The proof of the pudding is in the eating!

Traditional spaghetti sauce

You could leave out the can of tomatoes, but add an extra tablespoon of tomato paste. A small amount of chicken, pork or prosciutto could also be included.

2 tablespoons olive oil or butter

1 large onion, finely chopped

4 garlic cloves, crushed

1 heaped tablespoon finely chopped fresh rosemary

3 or 4 fresh basil leaves, finely chopped (optional)

6 mushrooms, finely chopped

5 skinned chicken giblets, finely chopped (optional)

½ skinned cacciatore salami, finely chopped (optional)

500 g rump, round or topside steak, finely chopped

2 tablespoons tomato paste

400 g can diced tomatoes

pinch mixed spice

salt and pepper, to taste

Heat most of the oil or butter (reserve 2 teaspoons) in a frying pan – preferably not a non-stick pan because you want to get a good browning on the bottom of the pan. Add the onion, garlic, rosemary and basil. Cook on low until the onion is soft and clear, and the bottom of the pan is slightly brown, but take care not to burn.

Meanwhile, soften the mushrooms in the reserved oil in a separate frying pan, then set aside.

Add the chicken giblets and salami (if using) and cook until brown. Add the steak, cook until brown. Stir in the tomato paste, tomatoes, spices and mushrooms.

Add just enough boiling water to cover the mixture (about 2 cups/500 ml), then partially cover the frying pan. Cook on low heat for 30 minutes, stirring occasionally, until nearly all the water is evaporated.

Serve over spaghetti cooked al dente, with a good sprinkling of freshly grated Parmesan cheese.

SERVES 4

South African braai (BBQ)

If ever there was a carnivorous race, it's the South Africans. When you go to a restaurant in South Africa and order a steak, half a beast comes delivered to you on a plate. You don't feel dissimilar to Fred Flintstone after he pulls away from the American Diner. Like the Americans, South Africans have big meals. In Australia, we love putting steak on the barbecue, burning it, then smothering it in tomato sauce before throwing it on a bread roll. But in South Africa, they are masters of marinating their meat, which enables them to cut down their cooking time and infuse delicious flavours into the meat. They are famous, too, for their sausages: boerewors.

Because the country has such rich grazing land, the quality of their meat and the way they prepare it is second to none.

Meat while on safari is truly supreme! It is part of the South African experience to get out in the bush, light a big fire and sit under the African skies. Then, when the fire dies down a bit, lie out a grill across it and cook meat that has been marinated for a long time.

The bush is an amazing place in South Africa. It is truly the great outdoors. I have been fortunate enough to have enjoyed some extraordinary safari experiences in Africa. One of the best was witnessing the migration of wildebeest across the plains. As these wildebeest reached the river crossings, there were crocodiles just basking in the sun or sitting there, still as logs, waiting to pounce on their fresh prey and drag them into the depths of the water. South Africa can be such a wild, unforgiving country!

In the morning, you rise before the sun and watch lions prepare for a vicious kill. You are on edge the whole time. You are in a car, but you are watching life unfold so incredibly close to you. The pecking order is well and truly established in that place!

In the evening, as the sun dips and the stars take over, it is a really special experience. Because South Africa is in the same hemisphere as Australia, the same stars can be seen. The Southern Cross is so striking in the sky.

Fire, with its warmth and feather-like flames, is a captivator. Those around it are drawn in, almost hypnotically, and beckoned to tell stories of truth, home and culture, and culinary delights are soon exposed. Like a moth is attracted to light so, too, are those around the fire enticed to talk.

South African braai (BBQ)

You could serve this with couscous salad or pesto pasta salad. Tomato, mozzarella and basil salad is also a favourite.

2 kg whole piece rump
1 garlic clove
2 cups (500 ml) red wine
½ cup (125 ml) olive oil
1 onion, chopped
4 bacon rashers, chopped
¼ cup (60 ml) soy sauce
2 cups (500 ml) BBQ sauce (smoky flavour)
10 large sprigs of fresh rosemary

Put the meat into a large glass or ceramic dish. Lay the side of a large knife blade on the garlic clove and flatten with the heel of your hand. Combine with the remaining ingredients (except the rosemary) and pour over the meat. Cover with plastic wrap and leave in the fridge for at least half a day, or up to 24 hours.

Drain the meat and reserve the marinade. Sear each side on a moderately hot BBQ plate. Turn the heat down to low, cover and cook for 2 hours. (I love the Weber or any BBQ with a lid to prevent meat from drying out during cooking. If you don't have one, you can cover the meat with foil.)

During this time, place the rosemary sprigs on the heat diffusers on the BBQ. This smokes and permeates the meat giving it an amazing flavour. Baste occasionally with leftover marinade.

Rest the meat for 15 minutes, before slicing to serve.

SERVES 6-8

Nicknames and favourite foods

Nicknames and food are specialities of the Aussie cricket team, so I thought I'd tell you a bit about them. My nickname is very simple – Haydos, which gets shortened to Dos. Jurassic, too, is another favourite (because they reckon I've got a big body and little head, much like a dinosaur!). My favourite meal is Kell's chicken casserole.

RICKY PONTING: Punter, because he bets on horses, dogs, fleas … anything! Punter loves his roast pork.

ADAM GILCHRIST: Gilly, and also Churchie. He gets called Churchie because after a tour game against Gloucestershire at Bristol Oval during the '97 Ashes Series, Adam bumped into a group of kids who, with great delight and eyes wide open, exclaimed to Adam, 'Ee, you're that Eric Gillchurch!' Gilly's favourite meal would be a toss up between penne arabbiata or Mel's stir fry Thai curry with the full monty of pappadums and condiments.

JUSTIN LANGER: Alfie, after Alfie Langer, the rugby league legend. We also call him Midge, as in midget, because he is so small. The boys reckon that Alfie is such a 'brown nose' that he'd say his favourite food is anything that I cook. (Harsh, Alf. Harsh! I know its Sue's seafood.)

GLENN MCGRATH: Because we reckon his legs look like a pigeon's, naturally we call him Pidge. He also gets called Mr Squiggle (after the old ABC TV children's character) since he's long and skinny like a pencil. Pidge's partial to anything that's been seared on a barbie.

DAMIEN MARTYN: Marto, for obvious reasons. His meal of choice would be steak and mushrooms: I have never known anyone who loves mushrooms as much as Marto!

SHANE WATSON: Watto, and Prince Charming from the movie *Shrek 2*, as he's the spitting image of him. Watto will eat anything – he'd be hard pushed to pick a fave dish!

SIMON KATICH: Katto, and Stiffy, because of his prolonged problems with a 'frozen' neck. Although Katto was born without the sense of smell, surprisingly he's retained his sense of taste and, like Watto, is such a good 'doer' on the food stakes. When I asked him about his favourite food, he replied, 'Mate, you'd have to go through the top ten not just one!' He finally narrowed it down to his old man's lamb on a spit with roast potatoes and steamed fresh green beans with loads of salt.

ANDREW SYMONDS: Simmo, and Roy, after the basketball star Leroy Loggins. He loves tucking into a T-bone with mashed potatoes and plain gravy, and for dessert he reckons his mum's lemon meringue pie is a bit of alright!

SHANE WARNE: Warney, SK, and The King. Margherita pizza would have to be his favourite when overseas, as he doesn't trust anyone on 'enemy' territory! On home soil he prefers to savour a Hawaiian pizza topped with very finely shredded ham, or hot chips on a bread roll with loads of butter and tomato sauce.

BRAD HOGG: Hoggy, and George. George is actually Hoggy's first name, but he can't stand it so goes by his middle name instead. He's a good country boy so meat and three veg is good to go for Hoggy – the plainer the better.

JASON GILLESPIE: Dizzy, after Dizzy Gillespie, the jazz master. However, we reckon our Dizzy is completely tone deaf, hence his love of all heavy metal rock bands! We've banned him from choosing the vibe music for the dressing room! Jason will tuck into bangers and mash with gusto every time.

BRAD HODGE: Dodgem, because of his love affair with the used car industry. Brad just loves spaghetti marinara.

MICHAEL CLARKE: Young Pup, and Milky because of his porcelain complexion. (Sorry, Pup!) He rates his mum's beef rissoles, mashed potatoes, veg and gravy as his all-time favourite meal, though tacos come a close second. One thing's for sure, Pup is always on the lookout for 'wingmen' to dine out at Mexican restaurants when on tour.

MICHAEL HUSSEY: Mr Cricket, because he is a complete and utter cricket tragic. Simmo reckons his favourite meal would be cricket ball sandwiches, but Mr Cricket claims it's spaghetti marinara!

BRETT LEE: Binga, after Bing Lee. He votes Weebix as his No.1 chow.

STUART MACGILL: Grape Juice, after his affection for a good bottle of vino. We also call him Robocop, because of his running style. He's rather fond of grass-fed Riverina beef fillet with truffled mash!

MICHAEL KASPROWICZ: Kaspa, Slobadam Smellavinavich and Salami Boy. There are a few more: Back Tank, Sub Tank, Fuel Tank, Bottom, after his well-rounded chaise. Kaspa loves a good antipasto platter, and just about anything that takes a long time to eat and enjoy, like a leisurely morning breakfast with great coffee and the daily newspapers.

Shabu-shabu

You will need a table-top cooker or clay pot with a burner underneath, as the cooking is done at the table. If you are keen, check out Asian supermarkets or speciality shops. I bought some of these back from my tour to Sri Lanka. An electric wok or frypan would do at a pinch. Ask your butcher about the best quality beef cut to use, and he may even slice it for you.

750 g beef fillet
¼ small savoy cabbage, shredded
350 g tofu, cubed
150 g fresh shiitake mushrooms, halved if large
1 cup (75 g) bean sprouts
30 g kombu seaweed
8 cups (2 L) veal or chicken stock
ponzu sauce or chilli soy sauce, to serve

Cut the beef into paper-thin slices. Arrange the beef slices, cabbage, tofu, mushrooms and bean sprouts onto a tray. Combine the kombu and stock in the heating vessel of your choice, and bring to a simmer.

Each diner takes some of the food in their chopsticks, and dips it in the simmering stock briefly to cook. They then transfer it to their own bowls. To eat, dip cooked food into the sauce of your choice. The leftover stock is served as a soup at the end.

SERVES 6

NOTE

If you part-freeze the beef fillet first, you'll find it easier to slice thinly

Tasty rib-eye with beetroot relish

MARINADE

4 garlic cloves, chopped

1 red chilli, chopped

1 onion, chopped

4 tablespoons olive oil

salt and pepper, to taste

BEETROOT RELISH

8 small beetroot, stalks trimmed

¼ cup (75 g) horseradish cream

4 rib-eye steaks, about 3 cm thick

12 stalks silverbeet

1 teaspoon butter

½ cup (125 ml) vegetable stock

Combine the marinade ingredients. Place the steaks into a shallow non-metallic dish, and pour the marinade over. Marinate for up to 1 hour, turning once.

To make the beetroot relish, cook the whole, unpeeled beetroot in a large pan of boiling water for about 20 minutes, until soft. Cool slightly, then slip the skins off and trim away the tops. Place into a food processor and process until pureed. Add the horseradish cream and mix well.

Tear the silverbeet leaves from the stems and roughly chop. Heat the butter in a pan and cook the silverbeet until wilted. Keep warm.

Cook the steaks in a heavy based frying pan for 3 minutes each side over medium high heat for medium rare. Set aside to rest, and add the stock to the pan and stir to take up the pan juices.

To serve, make a bed of silverbeet on each plate, place a steak on top and add a dollop of the beetroot relish. Drizzle the pan juices over the meat.

SERVES 4

Bangers and mash

This is a tribute to the grandparents of my wife, Kellie, and something to silence my Australian team-mate, Jason 'Dizzy' Gillespie. When I was talking with the boys, telling them I was doing a cookbook, an avalanche of rubbishing almost buried me.

Yet, when the dust settled and their attempted humour subsided, Dizzy said one thing was an absolute must for the book: 'You have to have bangers and mash in there, because you can't be an Australian without enjoying bangers and mash.'

When I first met Kell, the West Indies team was touring Australia, and Queensland was scheduled to play a match against them in Bundaberg. Kell thought it was an ideal chance for us to catch up with her grandparents who lived in the centre of good old Bundy.

Every morning delicious smells would waft by, as Kell's granddad cooked the best bangers and mash in town. It was a morning ritual. Kell's grandmother would go to daily Mass and her granddad would make you a cuppa, black with no sugar, like a good old bushie. Whichever grandchildren were visiting at the time would also bound out of bed and join in the tasty tradition of visiting the local baker for fresh bread, and then popping into the newsagent for the 'Bundy' Times. Then came the big breakfast.

As for most people of that generation, breakfast was a massive meal. It was kind of like the No.1 meal of the day. Well, Kell's granddad upheld that tradition! He would put these sausages in a tub of oil and fry the hell out of them. And then he would drain a little bit of oil out and make rich brown gravy. It was so nice, I can still taste it today!

In addition, he would make sure that before he cooked the breakfast, he went to the local bakery and bought a loaf of high-top white bread. He would cut slabs off the bread and dip into the gravy. What a feed! There we were, at 6.30 am, drinking black tea out of old teacups and eating bangers and mash.

Like all those bushies, he was wafer-thin! He was built like a stickman and had skin like leather, toughened from his years working in the steamy Bundy summer days on the railways. It was not a breakfast for the health conscious! But it was an epic, an old-fashioned treasure, that lives on in the memories of Kell and me.

Bangers and mash

3 cups (750 ml) beef stock
8 thick pork or beef sausages
2 tablespoons vegetable oil (or roast drippings)
1 tablespoon plain flour
salt and pepper, to taste
1 kg potatoes, peeled and chopped
1 tablespoon butter
3 tablespoons milk

Put the stock into a large saucepan and slowly bring to boil. When it is warm but not yet boiling, add the sausages. When the stock comes to the boil, remove the sausages. Keep the stock aside.

Heat the oil in a frying pan and add the sausages. Cook over medium heat until well browned and cooked through. (It's best to use a frying pan that isn't non-stick, because you want to get the sausages and the pan really brown, which makes a better colour and flavour for the gravy.) Drain the sausages on paper towels.

Return the pan to the heat. Add the flour and stir, scraping the bottom of the pan. Gradually add 2 cups (500 ml) of the reserved stock, stirring constantly to make smooth gravy. Season with salt and pepper to taste.

Meanwhile, cook the potatoes in a large saucepan of boiling water. Drain well, return to the pan and mash until smooth. Stir in the butter and milk, and season to taste.

Serve the bangers and mash with the gravy.

SERVES 4

Anything to pass the time

Another Test, another toss! Excitement all around — we're fired up and ready to confront the opposition. The umpires walk out, stoically. It's time! With a touch of our Aussie flag, a few warm-ups and a quick prayer, Alfie and I walk proudly to centre pitch. Alfie takes strike. A quick single. I prepare my wicket, do the usual housekeeping, take time to look around and, when I'm good and ready and have the opening bowler seething, I take strike. Another single. What was that I felt? Oh no ... rain! Back to the pavilion. It's pouring, coming down in buckets. The covers come out and we're cooked (jargon in keeping with theme of book!) till late in the afternoon. I knew you'd ask how we pass the time ...

Now, Michael Kasprowicz, Kaspa for short, my good Aussie teammate (even though he is a bowler) with fine Queensland blood flowing through his veins, always comes up with

something inventive and, while we were waiting to play in Mumbai, he had an idea that was a beauty. It even went international — to England, right through the Ashes series. It was called the Mumbai Mumbler and Kaspa became the in-house snitch journalist and editor-in-chief. Ruthless rumours, gossip and indeed anything at all untoward were collected methodically, filed meticulously, written ridiculously, edited unethically and flaunted flawlessly for all to read in the publication's change-room circulation.

Another time-passer: at the start of the World Cup Series tour, we all contributed to buying a good-quality team stereo to play our favourite music. Now, there was a slight problem: someone always had to carry the stereo onto the plane as it couldn't be packed in our luggage. It became quite a pain in the butt! We devised all kinds of games to sort out who would get the job. And so we had the scissors-paper-rock tournament – this was an elimination series so if you lost a round, you went back into the pool and if you won, you sat down. Finally, there would be one person who had to carry the stereo. If you didn't take the game seriously – chucking a third finger in, for example – that meant an automatic re-entry to the pool. You could take the rap to get a laugh, but you still remained in the running.

'Mozzie' Marbo (Jimmy Maher), another fine Queenslander, came up with one of the best games I've ever seen during the World Cup. Marbo has a great sense of humour and calls a horse race well. First, he devised names for each 'horse', or Aussie cricket team member, and he gave each runner a barrier. Then he organised a sweep. He went on to call the race, picking on the worst, funniest or silliest characteristics of each of us. 'And they're off! First out is the big-eared, old working mare from Perth [Gilly] …' He had us in stitches. Anything to pass the time!

Roast lamb shanks

Perth is lamb-shanks party time! A feast, the likes of which I have never seen before in a cricket ground dressing room. At the WACA there is a bloke called Go Go, employed to handle catering at the famous cricket ground. He is of Indian origin and runs a restaurant in Perth.

Besides the normal food offered at dinner breaks during cricket matches, Go Go does something absolutely amazing with lamb shanks. They are so delicious, I blame them for distracting me during a one-day match against India when I was dismissed for a duck!

Prime time 'feeding hour on the shanks' is typically after matches. If you want to perform at your best, you are not going to chow down on a massive lamb shank before or during a match. So no one really has the desire to stuff their faces before warm up, or during the innings, with lamb shanks. But at the end of the game, we are that hungry, and Go Go brings them in and there is a roar of approval from the boys. We are like a pack of sharks going through bait fish! Bits and pieces are flying everywhere! The shanks have been sitting there all day marinating in their own juice. These special shanks are so tender that you have to cup your hands under them in case meat falls from the bone – and you certainly don't want to miss out on eating all of the delicacy.

People can go nuts over all types of things – cars, boats and diamonds. We go mad over Go Go's delicious lamb shanks!

I said to Go Go one day: 'Go Go, before I hang up my bat and retire, I am not letting you go until you show me how you cook your lamb shanks.'

He gave me a book on Indian curries which he signed with the words 'God bless Go Go'. And he then taught me about dhal and the lamb shanks.

What I see in Go Go is one of the best gifts anyone can give me – the gift of sharing his knowledge. For me, he opened the door to an entirely new way of roasting food.

Roast lamb shanks

Serve the shanks with the vegetables and a pile of mashed potatoes to soak up some of the pan juices. Ask your butcher to french (trim) the shanks for you.

8 frenched lamb shanks

2 tablespoons grated fresh ginger

4 garlic cloves, crushed

1 teaspoon salt

1 large brown onion, chopped

1 large carrot, chopped

1 large celery stalk, chopped

Preheat the oven to 250°C. Arrange the chopped onion, carrot and celery into a baking dish to make a bed to roast the shanks on. Lay the shanks onto the vegetables and put into the oven for 5 minutes, to seal the meat. Take the tray from the oven and reduce the temperature to 180°C.

Combine the ginger, garlic and salt in a small bowl. Spread over the meat.

Pour 1 cup (250 ml) of water into the dish and cover tightly with a double thickness of foil. Bake for 2 hours, until the meat is very tender and falling off the bone.

SERVES 4

Pork salad with salt and vinegar peanuts

If you can't find salt and vinegar peanuts, there are other flavours you can get, such as balsamic vinegar, or chilli. You can even use plain nuts if you like.

MARINADE

1 tablespoon finely chopped ginger

4 garlic cloves, finely chopped

1 red chilli, finely chopped

1 tablespoon olive oil

$\frac{1}{2}$ teaspoon salt

$\frac{1}{2}$ teaspoon pepper

2 small pork fillets (about 200 g each)

1 cup (100 g) shredded red cabbage

$\frac{1}{2}$ iceberg lettuce, shredded

1 cup (75 g) bean sprouts

$\frac{1}{2}$ bunch coriander leaves, chopped

$\frac{1}{2}$ red onion, finely sliced

1 tablespoon olive oil, extra

1 tablespoon lime juice

1 cup (160 g) finely chopped salt and vinegar peanuts

Combine the marinade ingredients in a non-metallic dish and add the pork fillets. Cover and marinate for about 30 minutes. Cook on a hot BBQ, chargrill or frying pan for 10 minutes. Set aside to rest.

Place the cabbage, lettuce, bean sprouts, coriander and onion in a large bowl and toss to combine. Arrange onto serving plates or a platter. Thinly slice the pork and place on top of the salad. Drizzle with olive oil and lime juice, and sprinkle with the nuts. Serve immediately.

SERVES 4

Veal stew with parsley dumplings

I like to use an enamelled, cast iron casserole dish, which will go from the stove top to the oven (less washing up!). If you don't have one, you can cook on the stove in a large saucepan, then transfer the mixture to an ordinary casserole dish for the oven part.

½ cup (75 g) plain flour
salt and freshly ground black pepper
1 kg veal casserole steak, cut into 3cm cubes
¼ cup (60 ml) olive oil
2 onions, chopped
1 large carrot, chopped
2 stalks celery, chopped
4 garlic cloves, finely chopped
4 cups (1 L) vegetable or veal stock
1 cup (250 ml) red wine
2 sprigs rosemary

DUMPLINGS

2 cups (300 g) self-raising flour
40 g butter
1 cup parsley, chopped
salt and freshly ground black pepper
¾ cup (185 ml) water

Preheat the oven to 150°C. Season the flour with salt and pepper. Roll the meat in the flour to coat, and shake off the excess. Heat 1 tablespoon of the oil in a large (12-cup capacity) flameproof casserole dish. Cook the meat in 4 batches over moderately high heat until brown, adding more oil as necessary. Set aside.

Cook the onion, carrot, celery and garlic over medium heat for about 10 minutes, until they start to soften and become lightly golden. Return the meat to the pan along with the stock, wine and rosemary, stirring and scraping the bottom of the pan. Bring just to the boil, then place in the oven and cook, covered, for 3 hours, until the meat is very tender. Increase the oven heat to 200°C.

To make the dumplings, put the flour into a large bowl and rub in the butter. Stir in the parsley and salt and pepper. Add enough of the water to make a soft, slightly sticky dough. Carefully drop spoonfuls of the dough into the casserole. Cook uncovered for 20 minutes, until risen and lightly golden.

SERVES 6

Campsite delight

How much fun is it to sit around a campfire with kids and toast marshmallows? Grace just adores it. I love the outdoor life and the great thing is my kids do as well.

I reckon there are three wonderful things about a campsite:

- Fire. For some unknown reason, like a lot of blokes I have always had a strange infatuation with fire. I think there is something that opens up in your soul when you look into a fire and see the flames dancing and flickering in the night. Even its colours of orange, red and black fascinate me as they fuse together, change and grow brighter, then dimmer, and eventually fade to the burnt-out colours of charcoal.
- Toasting marshmallows.
- Camp ovens. The incredible ways you can control temperature and cook in them.

As a father, I believe there are so many simple lessons that can be taught to children at a campsite. For example, gathering timber to light the fire: it's important to gather just the right type of wood. It can't be too wet and it can't be too frail, otherwise it just ashes and blows away with the slightest breeze. How to be a hunter and gatherer. It's a bit like catching fish, really! There's something almost primitive about it, catching a fish and then preparing a meal on the open flame. Terrific! And it's also a great opportunity to teach kids about fire safety.

There's no better place to do these things than the beautiful Blue Lake on Straddie. It's a superb waterhole for swimming or for simply sitting around a campfire with family and friends, eating a delicious meal, relaxing and contemplating life.

Crumbed veal bake

This is a legendary dish around the campfire, with hot damper or a loaf of fresh bread to dunk into the sauce.2 tablespoons olive oil

2 onions, finely chopped

2 garlic cloves, finely chopped

2 red chillies, finely chopped

500 g ripe tomatoes, chopped

½ cup kalamata olives, pitted

salt and pepper

4 eggs

1 kg thin veal steaks (as for schnitzel), halved crossways

2 cups (200 g) packaged breadcrumbs

¼ cup (60 ml) olive oil, extra

1 cup (125 g) grated cheese

½ cup chopped flat leaf parsley

Heat the oil in a large saucepan and cook the onion and garlic until lightly browned. Add the chilli, tomatoes and olives, and cook, covered, on low heat for 1 hour. Season with salt and pepper to taste.

Beat the eggs in a large bowl. Working one at a time, dip the veal steaks into the egg then into the breadcrumbs to coat. Heat the extra oil in a large frying pan, and cook the veal in batches over medium heat, until browned.

Layer cooked veal and the sauce into a camp oven and top with grated cheese. Cover and stand at the side of your fire on a low heat. Heap hot coals onto the camp oven lid. Leave for 10–15 minutes to melt and brown the cheese. Uncover and top with parsley.

SERVES 6

NOTE

You can also cook this in a casserole dish in the oven, at 180°C for about 15 minutes

Vego

Caramelised onion and goat's cheese tarts

3 large red onions, peeled and cut into thin wedges

2 tablespoons olive oil

1 tablespoon brown sugar

2 tablespoons balsamic vinegar

salt and freshly ground black pepper

2 cups (300 g) plain flour

1 teaspoon baking powder

220 g frozen butter

6-8 tablespoons iced water

150g goat's cheese

Preheat the oven to 170°C. Combine the onion, oil, sugar and vinegar in a large baking dish. Season with salt and pepper. Bake for 45 minutes, stirring once during cooking, until tender and lightly golden. Cool completely.

To make the pastry, sift the flour, baking powder and a pinch of salt into a bowl. Grate in the frozen butter and shake through the flour to coat. Add the water, mixing through with a knife until evenly combined. Gather the dough into a ball. Wrap in plastic and chill for 30 minutes.

Preheat the oven to 220°C. Divide the dough into six equal portions, and roll each one out to a 15 cm round. Crumble the goat's cheese onto each pastry base, leaving a 3 cm bare border around the edge. Reserve some of the cheese. Spread the onions on top and sprinkle with the reserved cheese. Fold the pastry over to partially cover the filling.

Place on a baking tray and bake for 5 minutes, then reduce the heat to 180°C and cook for a further 30 minutes, until the tarts are crisp and golden.

MAKES 6

Spaghetti alla diavola

Diavola, meaning devil in Italian, refers to any dish which has been enlivened with chilli and garlic. This version is fairly mild, so add more garlic and chilli to crank it up if you like.

500 g dried spaghetti

1 cup (250 ml) olive oil

2 garlic cloves, peeled and sliced

1 teaspoon diced fresh chilli, or to taste

chopped fresh flat leaf parsley, to serve

freshly grated Parmesan cheese, to serve

Bring a large pan of salted water to the boil. Add a splash of oil and cook the spaghetti according to the packet instructions.

While the pasta is cooking, heat the oil in a pan over medium heat. Add the garlic and chilli and cook for 1–2 minutes, until the garlic starts to brown slightly. Drain the pasta and toss with the garlic and chilli oil.

Season to taste, and serve sprinkled with parsley and Parmesan cheese.

SERVES 4

Spinach and cheese triangles

You can substitute crumbled feta for the tasty cheese if you like, or use a combination of both.

1 bunch English spinach

2 eggs, lightly beaten

salt and freshly ground black pepper

4 sheets frozen puff pastry, thawed

1 ½ cups (185 g) grated tasty cheese

Preheat the oven to 200°C. Tear the stems from the spinach and discard. Wash and dry the leaves. Finely shred the leaves, and combine in a bowl with the eggs. Season with salt and pepper.

Cut each pastry sheet into four squares. Pile a little of the spinach mixture onto the pastry and sprinkle with cheese. Fold over to make a small triangle. Press with a fork to seal the edge, and prick a couple of holes in the top.

Place onto a baking tray and bake for 10–15 minutes, until golden brown.

MAKES 16

Incredible India

Unexpected things always happen in India. Whether it is the crowds at press conferences or at the hotel, or the different smells and sights, there's always something going on! There's a buzz in India because of the sheer size of the population.

One of the things I enjoyed most in the Travelex tour of India in 2004 was that it was split into two parts. The first and second Tests were back-to-back and then we had eight days off before the third and fourth Tests. During the break, I had the chance to fulfil some of my ambitions to travel in India. I set off with my good friend Jacob Cherian, an Indian who has been living in Australia for the past 20 years.

I had some incredible experiences. One of these was staying on a houseboat and cruising the backwaters of Kerala. They have an amazing way of life on the waterways. The only way people can get around is by boat. They travel to school by boat. They travel to church by boat. They get their food from the waters. Despite the difficult conditions they face in their daily lives, Kerala boasts the highest literacy rate in the world. Incredible!

Some of the photos I took on that trip say it all. I'm no photographer but I'm pretty happy with the cricket photo as, for me, it very much sums up the whole Kerala area. The Indians absolutely love cricket and in this area the kids were playing on this little strip – a patch of land ahead of a waterway, with rice paddies in the background and, to top it all off, a cow standing at fine-leg! It just tickled me.

Rice is the main source of income for the area and the paddies contribute to the beautiful scenery, awash with meandering canals as far as the eye can see. Visions of scenic north Queensland flashed into my mind as I quickly replaced the rice fields with cane fields. Frequented by Bollywood movie stars, the luxury houseboats, with their air-conditioned rooms, cooks, staff and servants, were something else!

A second incredible experience was going up into the mountains where Jacob's family owned a 3000-hectare tea plantation. Perhaps as a result of the area's colonial past, the homes of the wealthiest people are situated on beautiful hills. These overlook scattered small communities and the views are superb. Traditions are still strong and there is a timeless quality to the scene of women picking the leaves and carefully placing them into their baskets. Compared to the incredibly hot locations where we played cricket in India, the climate was cool, a real respite from the heat.

The food was cooked in Kerala's traditional style. It was eaten traditionally, too, with the fingers. I just love eating with my fingers. In India, it is the best way to experience the true texture of the different curries. All curries complement each other and they all feel so different. Nothing like a bolus of curry – yum! Absolutely delicious! And there were a lot of compliments when I ate with my fingers. 'Matt, we cannot believe you, a Westerner, eating as we do!' I have always believed that 'when in Rome, do as the Romans do'. It's a great way to get that feel for a different culture.

In the lowlands, among the water canals, there were fish curries. Prawn curries, too, were very popular. In the mountains, we were under instruction from an Ayurvedic masseur to eat a lot of fresh vegetables.

I love India – the people, the food, the places. And I'm really proud of the my role as a sports patron to the Global Public School in Kerala. I also love the fact that we in the Australian cricket team were finally able to climb our Everest, proudly hoist the Australian flag and say we had conquered the last frontier, India in India.

Avial

1 medium potato, peeled and thickly sliced
375 g green beans, trimmed and halved
2 carrots, peeled and thickly sliced
200 g green peas (fresh or frozen)
1½ tablespoons oil
2 green chillies, chopped
½ cup (85 g) grated fresh coconut
1½ cups (375 g) plain yoghurt
salt, to taste

Boil the potatoes, beans, carrots and peas until tender but still a little crunchy. Drain well.

Heat the oil in a frying pan and add the chillies, coconut and the vegetables. Whisk the yoghurt with salt to taste, and add to the pan. Mix gently and cook over low heat until warmed through. Do not boil.

Serve warm, at room temperature or cold.

SERVES 4

Bondas

You will need to go to an Indian speciality shop to get urad dal and asafoetida. If that isn't possible then leave them out. Besan (chickpea flour) is available from health food shops.

2 tablespoons oil

1 teaspoon mustard seeds

1 teaspoon urad dal

2 onions, sliced

4-5 green chillies, sliced

1 kg potatoes, cooked and mashed

salt, to taste

500 g besan (chickpea flour)

1-2 teaspoons red chilli powder, to taste

pinch baking powder

pinch asafoetida (optional)

salt to taste

2 cups (500 ml) water

vegetable oil, to deep fry

chutney or tomato relish, to serve

Heat the oil in a frying pan, and add the mustard seeds and urad dal. When the seeds begin to pop, add the onion and chillies and cook for a few minutes, until soft and lightly golden. Add the mashed potatoes, and salt to taste. Mix well and remove from the heat. Cool, then roll level tablespoons of mixture into small firm balls.

Combine the besan, chilli powder, baking powder, asafoetida and salt in a large mixing bowl. Make a well in the centre and gradually add the water, mixing to make a smooth batter.

Half fill a large saucepan with vegetable oil. Heat over medium high temperature. Dip the balls into the batter and fry a few at a time until golden brown. Drain on paper towels and serve immediately with chutney or tomato relish.

SERVES 6-8

Dhal

In 1998, a year before my Test recall into the Australian team, I pleaded with the Australian chairman of selectors, Trevor Hohns, to select me in a group of fringe Test players embarking on a development tour of India. The small squad included several spin bowlers and two batsmen, Matthew Elliott and Greg Blewett, who were bound for Madras under the tuition of former Indian spin kings, Bedi and Venkat. I caught wind of the trip and begged Hohns to allow me to go. I said I would even pay my own way over. I told him I had a very strong feeling that I would be part of something special over there, and I just wanted a chance to experience the conditions.

But Hohns said the book was full, although if there was another chance in the future, I would be considered. Two days later the phone rang. 'I have some good news for you,' Hohns said. 'Greg Blewett has pulled out.' I couldn't pack my bag quickly enough!

We stayed at the ground in Madras, a venue where, three years later, I was to score a Test century. The interesting thing was that when I was with the development squad at the ground, I said to Matthew Elliott, 'I reckon I'll get a Test match hundred here one day.' It was like the throwaway line prior to my first ever Sheffield Shield match when I said my aim was to make the highest score by a Queenslander on debut, which I did. It is amazing! It is something I really believe, that as you think, so shall you become – that what you think about pretty much manifests itself in life.

While in India, Sri Lanka and Pakistan, a day does not pass without having dhal. Dhal forms part of the staple diet on the sub-continent. It is what you eat, whether you have a million dollars or not a cracker. It is a very versatile meal. If you go to any restaurant or hotel, look at any menu or stop at any stall or market, you find dhal staring you in the face.

They cook it up in this big pot. Throw in coconuts, garlic, red chillies and water. Mix it up with tomatoes and that's it! They boil the hell out of it and away you go!

Even though I love seafood and meat, I also really enjoy the vegetarian food of the subcontinent. Dhal describes much about the subcontinent's culture. It is very deep and rich in colour, yet reasonably complicated because there is a lot you can do to it. Curl up your hands and use nature's tongs to eat it. It is either that or work for a year's salary to get some cutlery!

Vegetable Pakora

You will need to go to an Indian speciality shop to get ajwain; if you can't then leave it out. Besan (chickpea flour) is available from health food shops.

200 g besan (chickpea flour)
¼ teaspoon baking powder
2 teaspoons red chilli powder
2 teaspoons ground turmeric
2 teaspoons ajwain (bishop weed)
1½ teaspoons cumin seeds
salt, to taste
1 cup (250 ml) water
vegetable oil, to deep fry
1 potato, peeled and thinly sliced
1 capsicum, sliced
1 eggplant, sliced
1 onion, sliced
spicy tomato or green chilli sauce, to serve

Combine the besan, baking powder, spices and salt in a bowl, and make a well in the centre. Gradually add the water, stirring to make a batter.

Half fill a large saucepan with vegetable oil. Heat over medium high temperature. Dip the vegetables into the batter, and fry a few at a time until crisp and golden. Drain on paper towels, and serve immediately with the sauce of your choice.

SERVES 4-6

Vegetable Paratha roll

Chat masala is a spice mixture available from Indian speciality shops. Just leave it out if you can't get it.

500 g plain flour
good pinch salt
2 teaspoons oil
300 ml water
ghee, to cook

50 g beans, finely chopped
50 g carrot, finely chopped
50 g cauliflower, finely chopped
50 g cabbage, finely chopped
20 g butter or ghee
³/₄ teaspoon cumin seeds
1 onion, chopped
30 g red capsicum, chopped
20 g tomato, chopped
1¼ teaspoons ground cumin
1¼ teaspoons red chilli powder
³/₄ teaspoon chat masala
1 tablespoon chopped coriander leaves

Put the flour into a large mixing bowl, add the salt. Add the oil and enough of the water to make a dough. Knead gently just until smooth. Cover and set aside to rest.

Steam the beans, carrots, cauliflower and cabbage until just tender.

Melt the butter in a frying pan, and add the cumin seeds. When they begin to pop, add the onion and cook until translucent. Add the capsicum and cook for 10 seconds, then add the chopped tomato and cook for 15 seconds. Add the cooked vegetables and cook for 10 seconds. Stir in the ground cumin, chilli powder, chat masala and coriander leaves. Season with salt and mix well. Remove from heat.

Divide the dough into 5 portions. Roll out to a 23 cm round. Lightly grease a heavy based frying pan and cook the paratha one at a time for 2 minutes on each side, until golden brown. Roll the vegetable mixture in the paratha, and serve immediately.

SERVES 5

Let's hear it for the girls!

The debate raged after the Ashes loss. Why did we lose? Why? Could it be that the players' wives and partners ('the girls') were a distraction? Articles in the press asked this question, and have prompted me to give you an insight into the life of the girls to give you an idea of how they cope on tour and around Australian venues.

The girls have to be very special people. They are away from us for many months a year and, believe you me, touring for them isn't always beer and skittles. Kell once put it simply:

> The boys don't get a lot of spare time. Whatever time we get with them is worth it. Worth it for everyone – even a glimpse at breakfast! The priority is Matt when we tour so, with a young family, we get a separate room so he can have a good

night's sleep. We are in this life together and there is a need to understand his job and pressures, and to be there for him to break up his busy schedule. Being with him gives a sense of reality to our children, too. They need to understand his life, what he does.

In saying that it also gives our kids an amazing flexibility. They become used to travel, and meeting new people. They become very gregarious. The children of our 'cricketing family' are like brothers and sisters and, I guess, I'm like an 'aunt' to them. It's a difficult ask for little children to watch the game all day so, when possible, the girls, with or without children, all look after each other and plan excursions.

We are very fortunate in Australia. When we go to watch the boys, we are given private boxes where children have some roaming room and, in Melbourne and Sydney over the Christmas–New Year period, there is even a creche.

Sometimes it is a massive effort to even get to the grounds. In South Africa, it's not safe to jump in a taxi without security advice. It really all depends on the country. I remember, in England, when Matt was batting in the last Ashes Test, it took me two hours even to arrive at the ground and, with Josh still a baby, it was difficult. Then, at the ground, there were no facilities for us and we had to sit out in the sun. CA does provide facilities for touring wives/partners and children when they come to Australia, however. That's a really good thing for them.

I remember hearing from the boys after I had batted in Adelaide, when Kell was pregnant with Josh, that she had been thrown out of the SACA! Now, no one is more fastidious about dressing according to the standards of each ground and with her own great fashion sense than Kell. She always makes sure she checks on rules. She laughs, now, as she reminisces:

Oh, yes! How embarrassing! The girls were in a state of disbelief. I was six months pregnant with Josh and wore a long black skirt and very fashionable strapless top – certainly no bare tummy protruding. I was not allowed in! Sue Langer was with me and tried to plead my case but to no avail.

In the end, Kell went back to the hotel, changed and walked back.

That night, the media caught a sniff of what had happened. Kell was offered a gift voucher from a maternity shop in South Australia.

The days gone by were definitely harder for the girls and players' families, and they are certainly getting better. As for being a distraction, I can assure you there is nothing like having a wonderful, supportive wife and family.

Dessert

Apple crumble

You can vary this recipe by adding fresh or frozen berries to the apple, if you like.

800 g can bakers apple
1 teaspoon ground cinnamon
½ cup (90 g) sultanas
1 cup (150 g) plain flour
½ cup (115 g) brown sugar
¾ cup (70 g) desiccated coconut
125 g butter, chopped
ice-cream or double cream, to serve

Preheat the oven to 180°C. Spread the apple into a 5-cup capacity ovenproof dish. Sprinkle the cinnamon and sultanas over the apple.

Combine the flour, sugar and coconut in a mixing bowl. Using your fingertips, rub the butter into the dry ingredients to make a crumbly mixture.

Spread the crumble over the apple, and bake for 20 minutes, until brown. Serve hot with ice-cream or double cream.

SERVES 6

A cricketing Christmas

'*What are you up to for Christmas?*' It's a question often asked of me when I was playing international cricket. Christmas for me has been unique. It was so different from normal family celebrations, simply because it was like picking up home life and recreating it in a city that was on the eve of celebrating one of the biggest Australian sporting events of the calendar year – the Boxing Day Test. It was unique because I didn't travel home to those I loved and join in the festivities with them, they travelled to where I was – Melbourne, a city bursting with excitement, a city decked out in its best Christmas colours and buzzing with the anticipation of a well-planned, iconic sporting event.

So, what was different this particular year from the last? First, we were playing South Africa in the second Test. Second, we had been beaten in the Ashes series and there was speculation aplenty about the make-up of the team. Third, Alfie was injured and I had a new opening partner in Phil Jaques. And last but not least, the MCG had undergone an incredible revamp and was now one of the best sporting facilities in the world.

'*What actually happens on Christmas Day for you blokes?*' This was another of those regular queries. Usually, there's the team's preparation and meeting any new players. That Christmas, we all went to the ground for a hit and I familiarised myself with the environment. It's good for me to sit on the pitch and imagine what the stadium, filled with spectators, is going to be like on Boxing Day. Meeting Phil, my new opening partner, was important too: he was out of his comfort zone and I wanted to bridge that gap and settle some of his nerves. But that's another story.

Fitting Christmas in and around the Test match was always good. Because it was the only day of the year that Kell and the kids, and Mum and Dad got to be with me in the middle, it was special. It was so good to see them on the same ground that I was playing on the next day, and then to see the shenanigans of big Merv Hughes tackling Kell and tossing her over his shoulder and Gracey playing catch with Ricky Ponting as his wife Rianna looked on, laughing. Incidentally, I loved a photo of that moment so much it sat in my dressing room for the whole Test. Christmas – a time for kids? It's not bad for big kids, either!

Grandma's Christmas pudding

2 teaspoons baking powder

1 cup (250 ml) milk

185 g butter, melted

¾ cup (175 g) brown sugar

2 eggs, lightly beaten

3 tablespoons marmalade

2½ cups (375 g) plain flour

½ teaspoon each ground nutmeg, allspice and cinnamon

375 g packet mixed dried fruit

¾ cup (120 g) chopped dates

½ cup (70 g) chopped macadamias

6–8 pieces glace ginger, chopped

8 glace cherries, halved

1 cup (250 ml) rum

Dissolve the baking powder in the milk. Combine all the ingredients in a large bowl and mix until combined. Cover with plastic wrap and refrigerate overnight.

The next day, taste a little bit of the mixture and add more rum or spice if you like.

Grease a 2-litre capacity pudding bowl. Put the mixture into the bowl, and cover with a sheet of greaseproof or baking paper, and a sheet of foil. Tie securely under the rim of the bowl with a doubled length of kitchen string.

Stand the bowl on a wire rack or trivet in a large stockpot. Pour in enough boiling water to come ⅔ of the way up the bowl. Cover the pot and boil for 3 hours, topping up the water if necessary. Cool, then refrigerate until Christmas Day.

To reheat the pudding, boil the same way for 1 hour.

SERVES 8-10

Mum's chocolate and macadamia nut pudding

My mum, Moya, really is a good cook even if she doesn't think so!

Dad's favourite dish, made by Mum, is chocolate and macadamia nut pudding. It's one to die for!

As young kids, Gary and I used to sneak into the kitchen when Mum was cooking this dish, put our hands into the raw ingredients and pull out a fistful!

Today she tells us when we tease her unmercifully (but good-naturedly) about her cooking, 'Hang on! Wait a minute!' (We are always guaranteed to get a really good bite from Mum!) 'Where was my incentive?' she retorts. 'The raw ingredients were always gone – out the back door! Carried away on four healthy little legs before they even reached the oven! Anyhow … I have other talents!'

We have to agree with that. I'll even put it in writing.

Back to the dessert! It's really easy to make – hassle-free, simple and quick. (It has to be for Mum!)

The macadamia nuts are a must. The nuts come fresh from our Kingaroy farm. Out the back of the house we have a grove of macadamia trees and peach trees. The entire Kingaroy community is based around the nut trade. There would be about 20 or 30 macadamia nut trees that Dad planted when we were young fellas. These trees now produce more nuts than you can poke a stick at.

Dad collects the nuts and leaves them sitting on a piece of corrugated iron in a 'hold' shed. In summer, it gets so hot in that shed that the nuts almost roast. When it comes time to crack the nuts open, all these magpies that Dad has tamed gather around for the occasion.

I reckon Dad could tame a lion! He throws tiny pieces of nuts into the air and little willy wagtails swoop down and take the nut pieces before they can even reach the ground. Shouts of 'What a catch!' are often heard. Dad has all these magpies, too, eating out of the palm of his hand. He gives them a couple of nuts and carries the rest of the nuts to Mum who serves them with the chocolate pudding and ice-cream. Delicious, especially in winter!

I have come to realise that, unlike me, Mum and Dad are sweet tooths!

Any kind of occasion – birthdays, Christmas – Mum is always encouraged by Dad to ensure we have his favourite dessert on the Kingaroy family farm menu.

Mum's chocolate and macadamia nut pudding

Try this with a shot of your favourite after-dinner liqueur.

1 cup (150 g) self-raising flour
pinch of salt
2 tablespoons cocoa powder
³/₄ cup (160 g) raw sugar
¹/₂ cup (60 ml) milk
1 tablespoon melted butter
1 teaspoon vanilla essence
¹/₂ cup (70 g) chopped macadamia nuts
³/₄ cup (175 g) brown sugar
¹/₄ cup (30 g) cocoa powder, extra
1³/₄ cups (435 ml) hot water
vanilla ice-cream, to serve

Preheat the oven to 180°C.

Sift the flour, salt and cocoa powder into a bowl, and stir in the sugar. Add the milk, melted butter, vanilla essence and chopped nuts. Mix with a wooden spoon to a smooth dough, and spoon into a 6-cup capacity deep ovenproof dish.

Mix the brown sugar and extra cocoa powder together and sprinkle over the cake mixture. Carefully pour the hot water in at the side. Bake for 45 minutes, then let stand for about 5 minutes.

Scoop out into bowls with plenty of the sauce, and a big scoop of vanilla ice-cream.

SERVES 4–6

Blueberry surprise

Peter Robertson, the owner and winemaker at picturesque Brookfields vineyards and restaurant, is a long-time supporter of New Zealand cricket and he has had his fair share of touring sides visit his restaurant. After the fifth and final one-day international in New Zealand, the opportunity arose to get together with the New Zealand team and the boys jumped at it. Steve Bernard organised it. We had three spare days before we ventured up to Auckland for the start of the Test series. Luckily, for that trip I had Kell and Grace with me as well.

Brookfields is one of the oldest wineries in Hawkes Bay, and is situated between Napier and Hastings along the Tutaekuri River. Its attractive rose gardens and fine views of the vineyards make it just the right place for some quality time out.

Now, Simmo and Hoggy decided to go to the bowels of Brookfields' very impressive cellar, and returned in a slightly inebriated and jovial state. Just prior to dessert being served, Punter noticed Grace was playing with some Play-Doh on the grass.

Simmo had ordered a scrumptious-looking custard tart, served with fresh King Island cream from Tasmania and decorated with mouth-watering blueberries, which are beautiful around Hawkes Bay because the cool climate is ideal for them.

Punter had an idea. The colour of Gracey's Play-Doh was an almost-perfect match for the blueberries that garnished Simmo's dessert. He could see, too, that Grace was rolling the putty into small balls.

Hey presto! A quick replacement of blueberries with Play-Doh and the laugh was on Simmo!

Treacle sponge puddings

1 cup (150 g) plain flour
2 teaspoons baking powder
¼ cup (55 g) caster sugar
pinch salt
½ cup (125 ml) milk
40 g butter, melted
1 egg
few drops vanilla essence
¾ cup (185 ml) golden syrup
1 cup (250 ml) boiling water
hot custard, to serve

Preheat the oven to 180°C and grease six ¾ cup ovenproof dishes.

Sift the flour, baking powder, sugar and salt into a bowl. Combine the milk, butter, egg and vanilla in a jug (whisk with a fork to break up the egg), then add to the dry ingredients and gently mix until just combined.

Divide evenly between the dishes, and stand on a large oven tray.

Spoon a small amount of golden syrup carefully over the batter. Very gently pour boiling water over the mixture. Take your time so you don't disturb the mixture too much. It all looks a bit strange at this stage, but it does work! Bake for 15–20 minutes until risen and firm to a gentle touch.

Stand for 5 minutes, then turn out the puddings onto serving plates (use a folded dry tea towel to hold the dishes – they will be hot). Serve with custard.

SERVES 6

Simple pavlova

England would have to be Ricky Ponting's and Damien Martyn's dream country! Picture this – a lush English golf course, an inviting little two-storey villa overlooking the 17th tee and an historic bridge over a lake that reflects an old English castle in the background. Golf fanatics, Punter Ponting and Marto would have thought they had died and gone to heaven if they had stumbled into the house Northamptonshire provided Kell and me with during an English county stint.

I hate built-up areas so when I signed to play county cricket as Northants captain, a priority was where I was going to live.

Northampton is really a spillway from London, only 90 minutes up the M1 from the English capital. Not being a suburban kid, I need space, trees and some lawn. I need the fresh air and this place was a sanctuary! It had a lake for fishing, country living, excellent outdoor areas, plus a gym and a pool.

It was as great a place as any to have mates over and former English batsman, Allan Lamb, was front and centre in that regard. He is such a character, a real man's man, and his wife, Lindsay, is a magnificent cook.

Because of the English summer twilight, often you don't get to sleep until 11.30 pm, which gave Lamby and I time to train, then grab some irons and play a cheeky couple of holes in the fading light.

Lamby loves all the things that I love. He is a person who sees the lighter side of life and is one of cricket's great entertainers. Many a time he would put on a South African barbecue and we would bask in the afternoon sunlight with a special wine from his cellar.

Crawling before I walked in English cricket, I played league cricket first before entering the county scene. After my first Sheffield Shield season, I played at Greenmount, alongside Toombull's Chris Holding. In the Greenmount side, too, were Gary and Phil Neville of Manchester United and English National team fame.

The Nevilles were a wonderful family. They were particularly good to Chris and me, taking us into their home for meals. The boys' dad was named Neville Neville, of all things. He was chairman of the Berry Football Club.

Gary was my opening partner, a real mongrel dog! A competitor! Phil was younger and had more cricket ability. He could have played for England as a cricketer, but at that time the pair's football careers were just starting off and the money coming in for a soccer career was amazing.

Meeting people like the Nevilles was a sign of the quality of people who were to come into my English life.

Simple pavlova

2 egg whites

1½ cups (330 g) caster sugar

1 teaspoon cornflour

1 teaspoon white vinegar

1 teaspoon vanilla essence

3 tablespoons boiling water

300 ml thickened cream

fresh fruit, for topping

Preheat the oven to 160°C. Line a baking tray with a sheet of non-stick baking paper.

Place the egg whites, sugar, cornflour, vinegar, vanilla essence and boiling water in a large bowl, and beat with electric beaters until stiff peaks form. At first the mixture will be very runny but persevere, it will take a good 5 minutes to get to the right consistency.

Pile onto the baking tray, and use a spatula or the back of a spoon to smooth out to about 22 cm in diameter. Bake for 20 minutes, until lightly brown. Remove from the oven and let cool on the tray. Slide a large knife under the pavlova and carefully manoeuvre it off the paper-lined tray onto a serving plate.

Whip the cream and spread over the pavlova, then top with fresh fruit.

SERVES 8

What a week

There are many times in life when you are at a certain crossroads and, perhaps, you don't even know you are there until you are confronted with it. Then there are also times when you really need your wife, the person who knows you best and in whom you trust the most. That was how I felt before the final Ashes Test in England in 2005.

Even though I was too proud to say I needed my wife, I did. But the physical distance between England and Australia just seemed too huge: there was no way I was ever going to say to Kell, 'Look, I really need you here'.

I honestly couldn't believe it when I opened the door to my hotel room at 6.30 am. I will remember it forever. The image just blew me away.

At first there was a faint knocking, and sleepily I called out 'What?'

I really didn't want to get up early that morning; I was bone tired and just rolled over in bed. The knocking started again, more persistently this time. 'What is it?' I yelled loudly.

No answer.

A *very* loud, extremely persistent knocking started up and I thought, 'Aw, what? You have to be joking!' I shouted 'What is it?'

Even then, no answer.

So I shuffled up to the door and looked through the peephole. I saw a housekeeper. I opened the door, ready to unleash hell, especially as I had a 'do not disturb' sign on my door. Then, out of the corner of my eye, I saw little Joshy in Kell's arms. I was absolutely overcome with all kinds of emotions. What an incredibly wonderful sight.

That defined the week in a lot of ways for me. I mean, I was so euphoric that I had someone to share what was shaping up to be a really hard week. The knife was touching the heart; it was there ready to go. Kell and Josh's arrival gave me a pick-up that I can't describe. The result was that I felt such peace for the whole week in the lead up to the game, because I had my wonderful wife to share it with.

We lost the Ashes that week but, personally, I felt as though I had gained so much. First, I came through adversity and made 100 in that final Test. I saved my Test career. Secondly, I knew once again just how much sacrifice my beautiful wife was willing to make for me. And we had such an enjoyable week.

It's worth noting that lots of planets had to fall into line for our family to come together at that time. Travelling to England and then back to Australia with two young children would have been impossible. Mum and Dad and Kell's parents backed Kell all the way and had they not volunteered to have Grace, that wonderful surprise would not have eventuated. Their support was really special.

With a superb family and unbelievable support, you are the wealthiest person in the world.

Cakes & other sweet things

Honey-iced coffee cake

I have been extremely fortunate in my life, and I thank God every day for my many blessings. To wear the baggy green and be a part of such a great team – awesome! To travel the globe and play in venues all around the world – superb! To have the opportunity to experience other cultures and people from other countries – unbelievable! To make cricketing friends who remain great mates after cricket – the best! To get to know members of other cricketers' families – terrific!

It's well documented that I'm a big fan of Steve Waugh and his twin brother, Mark. They're both really good blokes, even though they come from 'Cockroach Country'!

Although they're twins, they get ribbed by the rest of us for not spending much time together. My belief is they just have very different interests. But one thing they most definitely have in common is they both love to eat.

Mark eats like he's just heard the starting jingle at Harold Park race track and needs to place a bet on a hot tip. Steve reminds me of a jackal on the plains of Africa, eating on the run, pick-pocketing a skerrick here and a skerrick there from old man lion's kill. Considering there are four Waugh boys in the family, I reckon that dinnertime at the Waugh house would've been as competitive as their legendary backyard cricket games!

Mark has a very dry sense of humour, and he really likes to look good – hence his nickname, Pretty! A cracking bloke, he calls a spade a spade. I'll never forget being at a meeting one day when Mark spoke out. It was a serious discussion about tactics and play when suddenly, in exasperation, Mark said, 'Just hit the ball! You're talking about crap! It's rubbish!' Nothing breaks up a group of fellas more than a statement like that, I can tell you!

Steve is a real family man. He loves a good joke as well as a good feed. We've often been partners in crime when it comes to seeking a decent meal. There's an unknown side, however, to this great Australian. His collar doesn't always match his cuff!

Steve's a tremendous practical joker and loves setting the stage for someone to make a fool of themselves. I'll always remember the morning after I'd made 380 and Channel 9's Steve Leibmann interviewed me. There I was, all set for a serious interview, but as soon as the cameras were turned on me I was pelted with mandarins, orange peel and apples. The moment we all cracked was when one of those massive exercise balls cannoned into the side of my head. Tracy Grimshaw couldn't contain her laughter but poor old Steve Liebmann was in a tight spot, trying to stay professional. It was impossible to concentrate with Steve whispering, 'Aren't you tired of talking about yourself yet, Haydos?'

When I dobbed him in, I knew no one would believe such an auspicious character as Steve Waugh would be up to such mischief. Yet he was just showing his true colours!

Steve truly has all the qualities most of us aspire to. However, his athletic abilities are almost insignificant when compared to his great sense of humanity, which I believe is his number-one asset.

My mate has a sweet tooth, and I know he prefers tea over coffee, but this next little sweet may change that preference!

Honey-iced coffee cake

If you can, use a shot of good espresso in place of the instant coffee. Serve with fresh flat whites and good friends.

3 teaspoons instant coffee powder

1 tablespoon hot water

125 g chopped butter, at room temperature

2 teaspoons vanilla essence

¾ cup (175 g) brown sugar

2 eggs

1 cup (150 g) self-raising flour

¼ cup (35 g) custard powder

⅓ cup (80 ml) milk

Honey Icing

30 g butter

1 teaspoon instant coffee

3 teaspoons hot water

1 teaspoon honey

1 teaspoon vanilla essence

1 cup (160 g) icing sugar, sifted

Preheat the oven to 180°C. Grease a 20 cm ring tin with melted butter, and line the base with non-stick baking paper. Dissolve the coffee in the hot water and combine in a large bowl with the butter, vanilla essence, sugar and eggs. Sift the flour and custard powder into the bowl and add the milk.

Using electric beaters, beat on low speed until the ingredients are combined, then increase speed to medium. Beat for about 3 minutes, until very smooth and lighter in colour. Spoon into the prepared tin.

Bake for about 30 minutes, until a skewer comes out clean when inserted into the cake. Stand for 5 minutes before turning onto a rack to cool.

When cold, transfer to a serving plate and spread with the icing.

To make the honey icing, melt the butter, then stir in combined water and coffee, the honey, vanilla essence and half the icing sugar. Gradually stir in remaining icing sugar until it's a spreadable consistency.

SERVES 8–10

The old school gate

Marist College, Ashgrove, in Brisbane, was a gateway for me. The school's motto says it all: 'Viriliter Age', which translated means 'to act manfully'.

Two things stand out in my mind about the school – city life and discipline. As a country fella, I had to leave the home I loved so much and become a boarder. Marist College meant I was living in the city, which was a really different experience. After the easy-going lifestyle in the bush, the comforts of home and the lack of discipline, I had to get used to the 'super-structure' of boarding school life – what time to study, what time to go to sleep, what time to eat, what time laundry had to be in, what time to have a shower … I could go on and on! I also had to learn how to cope with socialising in groups and to fit in with a culture that was different from home. I found many of those new things very, very confronting – but I learnt many things, not only about other people but also about myself.

I will always remember waking up on my first morning there. I was absolutely starving! (Food was always plentiful at home.) I found myself saying to anyone at all: 'Hey, mate, where's the food hall? Where's the mess?'

One boarder answered, 'Oh, no, no, no, no! It's not open till [whatever time it was]. You have to have a shower first and put on your uniform.' He and the other boarders gave me the lowdown.

Well, I'll tell you what, I was first showered, first dressed and definitely first to reach the food hall.

And there I saw, like the Holy Grail sitting on top of the table, this huge jug of milk. Well, that was gold! I loved milk, and thought: 'You beauty! This boarding school's not too bad after all.' So I helped myself. After I had drunk three or four glasses and eaten a couple of bowls of cereal, the rest of the blokes came in and sat down at the table. I discovered someone was the leader, and he was looking a little perplexed. He started measuring the remainder of the milk left in the jug, dividing out a ration (a word unfamiliar to me and my former lifestyle) of one cup to each boarder. But by the time the third cup was poured out, there was not a drop left. The boys were looking for answers. And I was sitting there as happy as a fat spider! The fact was I had tucked in to half a cow!

Well, it wasn't a particularly good start that morning. I made a bluey! But I didn't know, did I? The next day wasn't very pleasant. I had a table all to myself! I had learnt the hard way. But as time passed, I started to enjoy the culture, particularly in my senior year, Year 12. I was a little more settled and understood the system more. I also understood when to buck and when not to!

To this day, I have very fond memories of Ashgrove and always, ahead of the first club game of the year at Valley's Cricket Club oval, I go up to the school, alone, and say a little prayer in the Marist College Chapel. It's only a small, private chapel but it's right at the very heart of the school. It's a nice time, 20 or 30 minutes when I can sit and contemplate on my past years, and reflect, too, on the boy I was – that young bloke from the country, who had a wonderful opportunity, thanks to the sacrifice of his parents. That Matthew Hayden was a young, country teenager who, in some ways, probably took that opportunity for granted, but he now knows how lucky he was to have such a great 'school tie'.

When I first arrived I had to open 'the gate' of Ashgrove's Marist College. It led to another road on my journey of life when I had to close that gate and walk out into the real world. Now, I hold my head up high and remind myself, daily, of the school's wonderful motto, 'to act manfully'.

Passionfruit and coconut cake

This big cake is great for feeding a crowd.

150 g butter

1¹/₂ cups (330 g) caster sugar

4 eggs

2 cups (300 g) self-raising flour

1 teaspoon baking powder

2 cups (180 g) desiccated coconut

¹/₂ cup (125 ml) milk

¹/₂ cup (125 ml) passionfruit pulp

ICING

3 cups (480 g) icing sugar

50 g softened butter

2 tablespoons passionfruit pulp

1¹/₂ tablespoons hot water

Preheat the oven to 180°C. Grease a 25 cm round tin with melted butter, and line the base and sides with non-stick baking paper.

Using electric beaters, beat the butter and sugar until creamy. Add the eggs one at a time, beating well in between.

Sift the flour and baking powder together, and combine with the coconut. Fold into the butter mixture in 3 batches, alternating with the combined milk and passionfruit pulp.

Pour into the cake tin, and bake for about 45 minutes, until springy to a gentle touch. Leave in the tin for 5 minutes then turn out onto a wire rack to cool.

To make the icing, beat all the ingredients together until creamy. Spread over the cooled cake.

SERVES 12

Orange ring cake

This has to be the quickest and easiest cake ever made.

60 g soft butter
1 cup (220 g) caster sugar
2 eggs
1 tablespoon orange juice
1 teaspoon finely grated orange rind
2 tablespoons milk
½ teaspoon vanilla essence
1½ cups (225 g) self-raising flour
sifted icing sugar, to decorate

Preheat the oven to 180°C. Lightly grease a 20 cm ring tin and line the base with non-stick baking paper.

Place all the ingredients into a bowl, and using electric beaters mix on low speed until combined.

Increase the speed to high and beat for 2 minutes only. Pour into the tin, and bake for 30 minutes, until the cake springs back to a gentle touch. Leave to stand in the tin for 5 minutes. Run a knife around the outside and inside ring of the cake, and turn out onto a wire rack to cool.

Put some icing sugar into a small fine sieve and dust over the top of the cake before serving.

SERVES 8

Coffee cheesecake

There is nothing my mum and dad have not done for me, and their commitment to my life has been a major reason for my success.

There was a time when I was happy simply to follow in the footsteps of my father, grandfather and great-grandfather by farming our property at Kingaroy. As a youngster, I loved leaping into the tractor cabin, putting on ABC radio and working the land. Dad and I would cross each other in the field and give each other a wave as we went. I wanted nothing else in life!

Even today, when we go home to the farm, it gives me great pleasure to see my beautiful daughter, Gracie, riding on a tractor with Dad, and being showered with love by both Mum and Dad.

I can still hear Mum and Dad saying at different times, 'Matt, you can always come back to the farm if you really want to, but you must get an education first.' Both Gary and I knew we had to have a secondary education and then go on to university.

Mum and Dad encouraged me to follow Gary to boarding school at Marist Brothers College, Ashgrove, where my schooling and cricket benefited.

Distance was no barrier for my parents, even though at times they were hundreds and hundreds of kilometres away in Kingaroy. They have always been prepared to drop anything in support of their family. Dad bought his old Statesman from Sir Joh, or at least from the Premier's Department, and it has done the rounds!

As a young lad, when I was selected to play representative cricket, the kilometres that were covered were incredible. Sundays during the cricket season were spent travelling to Gympie, Bundaberg, Maryborough, the Sunshine Coast, Hervey Bay or Biggenden. An early start of around 5 a.m. was essential and often we would not get home until around 9 or 10 p.m. That was only at Wide Bay level – many more kilometres were added at Queensland level!

That old car carted me from one cricket match to another as a kid, and when I first started playing for Australia, Mum, Dad and Gary jumped in the car and followed me around the country. To this day they think nothing of driving three hours if Kell needs a hand while I am away. They have been everything to me and the opportunities they have given me have made me the person I am today.

They have followed me to England when I played county cricket – though not in the Statesman! It was in England that Mum and Dad stumbled upon the finest dessert they have tasted – courtesy of Dad's cousin, Jim, and his wife, Helen.

The four were in England staying with us and Helen produced her classic dessert, coffee cheesecake, that was a huge hit. I am not a great sweets lover, but it was divine. It remains one of Mum and Dad's favourites, and with good reason.

Coffee cheesecake

250 g packet milk arrowroot biscuits

3 teaspoons drinking chocolate

1 tablespoon instant coffee powder

125 g butter, melted

3 eggs, separated

3 tablespoons instant coffee powder

1 teaspoon vanilla essence

½ cup (125 ml) milk

¼ cup (60 ml) hot water

1 tablespoon gelatine

500 g cream cheese, at room temperature

1½ cups (330 g) caster sugar

300 ml whipped cream, to decorate

drinking chocolate, to dust

Put the biscuits into a food processor and process until they form crumbs. Add the drinking chocolate and coffee powder and process briefly to combine. Add the melted butter and process until well combined. Spread out into a 24 cm springform pan, pressing firmly with the back of a spoon or the bottom of a glass to pack down the base. Put into the fridge while you make the filling.

Mix together the egg yolks, coffee powder, vanilla essence and milk. Put into a small saucepan and stir over a very low heat for about 5 minutes, to make a custard. Don't let this mixture boil. Transfer to a bowl to cool slightly.

Put the hot water in a small bowl and sprinkle the gelatine evenly over it. Leave for a few minutes to soften, then whisk with a fork to dissolve.

Put the cream cheese and ½ cup (110 g) of the sugar into a bowl and beat with electric beaters until smooth and creamy. Add the custard and the gelatine mixture, and beat to combine.

In another bowl, beat the egg whites until stiff, then gradually add the remaining caster sugar, beating constantly. Fold this into the cream cheese mixture and pour over the base. Put in the fridge to set for about 6 hours – but it is best made the day before.

Before serving, top with whipped cream and dust with drinking chocolate.

SERVES 10–12

Australian sons

I once heard the saying 'the strongest steel goes through the hottest fire', and its significance really hit home on our momentous visit to Gallipoli. Just before the 2005 Ashes tour, the Australian one-day team was given an insight into more courageous exploits of the Anzacs. In Villers-Bretonneux, near Amiens in France, we were proud to call ourselves 'Australian sons'. We were so privileged to be able to immerse ourselves, although too briefly, in the emotions of that once war-torn French village and to understand why there still exists a debt of honour and gratitude to those fearless, heroic Diggers.

Steve Waugh initiated the tradition of visiting battle sites of Australian war history and the tour, organised in conjunction with the Australian Army, took us to two places. First we went to the National Australian Memorial. This is an impressive memorial commemorating the 10,982 Australians who died in France and who have no known grave. We also went to the Franco-Australian Museum, housed in the roof of the Villers-Bretonneux school, which was rebuilt with the aid of funding from the State of Victoria in Australia, and money donated by Victorian schoolchildren whose fathers, numbering 1200, are buried in the Villers-Bretonneux cemetery. Sadly, there are many more names inscribed on the memorial.

Our trip there was rushed. We arrived at Heathrow in London, tracked across by train to Lille, went straight out to the war memorial, then visited the school, had lunch at Le Kangaroo, went back to Lille that night and then left the next night, by train, back to London. So we got a snapshot of the Battle of the Somme. Because of the time restraints, I wasn't able to become as absorbed by the significance of that hideous battle as I was by Gallipoli, when we visited there. On that visit, we had almost two full days on the peninsula, the whole of which is, in effect, a huge war memorial. It is untouched – rocky headlands, the lot. In France, life has gone on. The towns are busy. Time has not stood still. So, apart from the old, tell-tale trenches in the war-memorial sites, it was a little difficult to get that genuine feeling of war, especially as our visit took place in the height of summer. I believe this is a good thing. It is wonderful that towns in the Somme have been able to get on with life while people can still visit memorials to commemorate and say prayers for those brave soldiers who gave their lives, the supreme sacrifice, so that others might be free.

In some countries we visited, there were kids who were dramatically affected by war every day of their lives. Yet in France, kids were kids! They asked for autographs and although there was a language barrier, that didn't matter. They laughed. They played. They were happy. They were free spirits. That is the legacy of our forefathers, the Anzacs. Inside the school hall is an inscription that reads: *N'oublions jamais l'Australie*. It means, 'Let us never forget Australia'. I was overwhelmed with a tremendous sense of pride, not only for the honour and gratitude given to the Anzacs, but also to see how almost 100 years later the lives of the Villers-Bretonneux people have been affected, forever, by great Australians with great fighting spirits and great qualities.

As an Australian athlete, it's an incredibly uplifting experience to visit these places and to know the same Australian blood is running through my veins.

I salute you, Anzacs (and all Australian forces, past and present). I, as an Australian son, rejoice and take great pride in recognising your heroic achievements.

Anzac biscuits

1 cup (100 g) rolled oats
1 cup (150 g) plain flour
1 cup (220 g) caster sugar
³⁄₄ cup (70 g) desiccated coconut
125 g butter
1 generous tablespoon golden syrup
1½ teaspoons bicarbonate of soda

Preheat the oven to 160°C. Line baking trays with baking paper.

Place the oats, flour, sugar and coconut into a large bowl and stir to combine. Melt the butter and golden syrup in a saucepan. Put the bicarb into a cup, add 2 tablespoons of boiling water and stir to dissolve. Stir into the butter mixture until frothy, then add to the dry ingredients and mix until evenly moist.

Roll level tablespoons of the mixture into balls and place onto the baking trays (you will probably have to cook them in batches). Flatten out slightly with your fingertips, and make sure you leave room for spreading. Cook for about 12 minutes, until flat and golden brown. Leave on the trays for 5 minutes, until firm, then transfer to a wire rack to cool completely. Store in an airtight container – do not eat all at once!

MAKES 36

Buttermilk pancakes

I absolutely love these served with maple syrup and smoky bacon. I got used to the sweet and savoury combination while on a skiing holiday in Vermont, USA. A bad habit, I know, but I figured 6 hours of skiing a day would be enough to burn these babies off!

2 cups (300 g) plain flour
2 teaspoons baking powder
1 tablespoon caster sugar
pinch salt
2½ cups (625 ml) buttermilk
2 eggs, lightly beaten
80 g butter, melted and cooled slightly
maple syrup, to serve

Sift the flour, baking powder, sugar and salt into a bowl. Add the combined buttermilk, eggs and butter and mix together to a smooth batter.

Lightly grease a heavy based frying pan. Pour ⅓ cupfuls of the batter into the frying pan and cook over medium heat. When bubbles appear on the top, turn over and cook the other side for 1 minute.

To make blueberry pancakes, scatter blueberries over the uncooked side before flipping.

Serve with maple syrup.

MAKES 10

Lemonade scones

Last time I made these I had Josh balancing on my hip — it's just that easy. Mind you, he looked like a rat out of a flour bin by the time we finished!

4 cups (600 g) self-raising flour
1½ teaspoons baking powder
300 ml lemonade
300 ml cream

Preheat the oven to 220°C. Sift the flour and baking powder into a bowl, then add the lemonade and cream. Mix lightly until evenly combined.

Pat out on a lightly floured surface until about 4 cm thick. Cut out 9 cm rounds. Place onto a lightly floured oven tray and bake for 20 minutes, until puffed and golden.

For sweet scones, add ½ cup sultanas or chopped dates and 2 tablespoons caster sugar.

MAKES 9–10 SCONES

Melting moments

185 g butter, softened slightly

¹/₂ cup (80 g) icing sugar

1 teaspoon vanilla essence

³/₄ cup (115 g) plain flour

¹/₂ cup (75 g) cornflour

Butter cream (optional)

60 g unsalted butter

1 teaspoon vanilla essence

1 cup (160 g) icing sugar

Preheat the oven to 160°C. Line baking trays with non-stick baking paper.

Place the butter into a bowl, and sift the icing sugar over. Using electric beaters, beat until creamy. Add the vanilla and beat until combined.

Sift the flour and cornflour onto the butter mixture, and stir until combined. Roll heaped teaspoons of the mixture into balls and place onto the prepared trays. Flatten gently with a fork (dipped in flour to prevent sticking).

Bake for 15 minutes, until just pale golden. Leave on the trays for 5 minutes, until firm, then transfer to a wire rack to cool completely. Sandwich the biscuits together with butter cream, if you like.

To make the butter cream, beat the butter, vanilla and sifted icing sugar together until creamy. If you want you can flavour the butter cream with finely grated orange rind, coffee, or almond essence.

MAKES 36 OR 18 DOUBLES

Vanilla slice

Travelling as a member of the Aussie Cricket team, I vividly recall sitting beside a curious American who worked for the Ford motor vehicle company in Detroit. We started swapping small talk and, suddenly, his curiosity got the best of him.

'What's with the uniform man? Ya in some sorta team?'

'Yes, mate. I'm an Australian cricketer,' I answered proudly.

'Yeah?' he drawled. 'Now, there's one game I just don't get.'

At that moment I knew I was in for a long stay at the crease! Using baseball as an analogy, I explained, as simply as I could, the finer points of the game.

Periodically, he interjected. 'What? Get outta here! Ya mean ya play the game for five days and not get a result? What's the fun in that, man? Ya don't even get a winner or a loser! Damn! That's like kissing ya sister!'

My travelling companion was not to be deterred. I had the feeling this would be a long flight! A puzzled look, at times, appeared on his face but he pushed on, still trying to get the gist of the game.

'Now, let me see if I've got this. Ya say the game can last for five days and ya can be in a room with most of ya team for sometimes two whole days, just sittin' around?' He stopped and shook his head. Then, sitting upright, he added quickly, 'Jeepers, man, whadda ya talk about in that time?'

I laughed and went on to tell him all manner of things are discussed. Of course, assessing the game is the most important, but many topics of conversation are put forward for non-serious discussion, too.

'Yeah! Like what?' he mused.

'Well, mate, topics like, who would make up The Most Talented Aussie Team, or The Ugliest Cricket Team in the World, or The Wankers Eleven ... All manner of things get ranked and talked about.'

He chuckled and added, 'You Aussies! Ya sure have a good sense of humour!'

Then, in a hushed tone, he continued, 'Do they feed ya, man?'

And so the conversation turned to food. I explained that the Australian team is very progressive in its approach to our diet, and that dietitians are employed to manage and give pertinent advice on the food we eat.

That exchange with my American companion led me to reflect on the food I've eaten at cricket grounds, from my early days at my beloved Brisbane Gabba, where I feasted regularly on a huge eye-fillet steak with chips; to my county cricket days in England where traditions were still followed by players like David Gower, who drank a cool Chardonnay with his lunch; and to Lord's, which boasts, rightfully so, of one of the best restaurants on the planet. 'Tea' was served in that wonderfully traditional English manner, with sandwiches, muffins, scones, jam rolls and other delicious sweet treats.

As Allan Border says when he wanders around the dressing room after 30 years of superb service to the game, 'Whatever happened to the good old days?' Being a lover of food, I must admit that I, too, miss those days when I could tuck into a wicked little treat!

The best treat I ever had was in 1997, when I was a pro for Hampshire County Cricket Club. They served these unbelievably delicious vanilla slices on trays at teatime. When it was cold and wet, the combination of the chilly English weather and the aroma of freshly made vanilla slices really tested my discipline. Let's see if they test yours as well!

As for my American friend and cricket ... well, I'm sure he still doesn't get it! He was a good bloke, though, and our chat did kill some time on the flight. Even better, we had a good old laugh.

Vanilla slice

So simple but tastes soooo good!

2 sheets puff pastry
300 ml thickened cream
2 x 85 g packets instant vanilla pudding mix
2 cups (500 ml) milk
1½ cups (185 g) icing sugar
1 tablespoon soft butter
2 tablespoons boiling water

Preheat the oven to 180°C.

Put the pastry sheets onto two lightly greased baking trays and prick all over with a fork. Bake for 20 minutes, until they are puffed and golden brown. Remove from oven and set aside to cool.

Using electric beaters, whip the cream until soft peaks form. Put the vanilla pudding mix into another bowl and, using a wire whisk, stir in the milk.

Quickly fold the whipped cream into the pudding mix, then spread over the top side of one of the pastry sheets. Put the other sheet on top, flat side up.

Sift the icing sugar into a bowl and stir in the butter and water. Spread over the top of the slice. Leave for about 10 minutes, for the icing to set. Cut with a serrated knife into 12 pieces, and keep stored in the fridge.

MAKES 12

The heat is on!

When you talk about heat in a cookbook, it is usually associated with the temperature of the oven. But in this story heat refers to the pressure all Australian batsmen come under when they don't consistently score runs. The reality is that cricket is about performance. And when you are not performing, you need to look over your shoulder.

However, there's an element of 'doing it your own way' and of 'sticking to your own game' that ultimately lays the foundation of your performance. In my experience, every time I've got into trouble it's generally when I have been trying to prove someone wrong, or when I've tried to change my game to be like someone else's. Don't get me wrong, I would love to have been like Steve Waugh! His game was flamboyant through the covers, stylishly played, but the reality is I'm not like him. I play the way I play and the greater attention I pay to the detail of sticking to that, the better I perform.

I find it handy to say to myself, 'Next ball'. It doesn't matter about a ball in the past. It doesn't matter about some other future ball. It's simply the next ball. That raises a question of balance, I believe. When you are under pressure, you have to put things into perspective because, as a professional cricketer, there is one thing for certain: you are going to have disappointments. Luckily, I have had my fair share of disappointments and in those I have always seen great lessons and opportunities. I have turned those disappointments around, and focused on getting better, not bitter.

The inscription down the stringer on my surfboard says it all: 'Endless Progression'. When I look at those words, they fill me with optimism, purpose and, ultimately, balance. I try to apply this philosophy to everything I do, including my family life, cooking, surfing, fishing, and my relationships with friends, colleagues and business associates. I try to look at life from that perspective.

There are times in life, too, when you have to know when to push on politely – attack is not always the best method of defence in terms of the subtleties of relationships, but the strength of character and the inner resolve to acknowledge that perhaps someone has a point is. In the end, no one will remember the centuries you've made, the five-fours you've achieved or the catches you've taken; what they will remember is how your character was revealed in whatever it was you did – and in my case it's cricket.

Acknowledgements

Family is the cornerstone of the 'Hayden Way of Life'. On so many levels, Kellie, Grace, Josh and Tom have enabled and empowered me to experience a fabulous life full of rich and meaningful journeys. I want to thank them all for their infinite patience, sacrifice and love. May our journey continue till our cup 'runneth over'.

My cricketing journey was acknowledged for a fact I am very proud of: the ability to build successful partnerships. ABC Books, now joined with Harper Collins, have been a beautiful extension to those partnerships off the fields of cricket and into the kitchens of the world.

In particular, I would like to thank Brigitta Doyle and her amazing team for their tireless efforts. You have all made my first touch with publishing an extremely enjoyable experience.

To all those people who have used these books as a way to engage and promote family, friends and community through our mutual love of food, thank you. It has been my pleasure and delight to mix together the ingredients of family, friends and love, blended with yarns and adventures across our planet, and then produce a final product to share a little taste of our lives with you.

Index

A

aioli 49
Anzac biscuits 269
apple crumble 231
asparagus chicken casserole 130
avial 215
avocado and mango salad 12

B

bangers and mash 189
batter, beer 89
Baxters salmon quiche 46
beef
  rib-eye with beetroot relish 184
  rissoles 171
  shabu-shabu 183
  South African braai (BBQ) 179
beer battered flattie 89
biscuits
  Anzac 269
  melting moments 274
bondas 217
bruschetta 22
bug tails with mango salsa 59
buttermilk pancakes 270

C

cake
  coffee, honey-iced 255
  passionfruit and coconut 258
  orange ring 261
calamari 62
calypso crayfish 76
camembert dream pie 27
caramelised onion and goat's
  cheese tarts 207

cheese and spinach triangles 211
cheesecake, coffee 264
cheese pie, camembert 27
cheese risotto 38
chicken
  crispy 135
  macadamia and feta stuffed 143
  pie 146
  tikka 154
  curry 151
chicken casserole, asparagus 130
chilli lime aioli 49
chilli Mumbai lagoon crabs 67
chocolate and macadamia nut pudding 239
Christmas pudding 234
chutney, mango 52
coffee cake, honey-iced 255
coffee cheesecake 264
coral trout Thai style 73
crab lasagne 68
crabs, chilli 67
crayfish, calypso 76
crispy chicken 135
crumbed snapper 123
crumbed veal bake 202
cucumber salad 17
curry, chicken 151

D

dressings and sauces
  balsamic dipping sauce 81
  chilli and lime aioli 49
  chilli and lime dipping sauce 96
  roasted garlic aioli 49
  salad dressing 12
  yoghurt dipping sauce 81
dumplings, parsley 199

F

fish pie 84
flathead, beer battered 89
fried fish with two sauces 81

G

Gabby's lasagne 161
Grandma's Christmas pudding 234
Grandma's shepherd's pie 164
gumbo, seafood 110

H

honey-iced coffee cake 255

K

Kell's asparagus chicken casserole 130
KP meat pie 168

L

lasagne, sandcrab 68
Lasagne (meat) 161
lemonade scones 273

M

macadamia and feta stuffed chicken 143
mango and avocado salad 12
mango chutney 52
mango salsa 59
Matty's mussels 92
mayonnaise see aioli
meat pie 168
melting moments 274
mussels 92
Mum's chocolate and macadamia nut
  pudding 239

N

Nola's chicken pie 146
noodles, pad Thai 95

O

orange ring cake 261

P

pad Thai 95
pakora, vegetable 222
paratha roll, vegetable 225
parsley dumplings 199
passionfruit and coconut cake 258
pancakes, buttermilk 270
pavlova 246
pie
  camembert 27
  chicken 146
  fish 84
  meat 168
pizza
  prawn 30
  Straddie 35
pork salad with salt and vinegar
  peanuts 196
prawn and scallop skewers 102
prawn pita pizza 30
prawn rice rolls 96
prawn salad, udon 99
pudding
  Christmas 234
  chocolate and macadamia nut 239
  treacle sponge 243

Q

quiche, salmon 46

R

red emperor, salt encrusted 107
rib-eye with beetroot relish 184
risotto, cheese 38
rissoles 171
roast lamb shanks 195

roasted garlic aioli 49
Roy's calamari 62

S

salad
  avocado and mango 12
  cucumber 17
  pork, with salt and vinegar peanuts 196
  udon prawn 99
salmon quiche 46
salsa, mango 59
salt-encrusted red emperor 107
sandcrab lasagne 68
sauces *see* dressings and sauces
sausages and mash 189
scallop and prawn skewers 102
scallops with coconut rice 115
scones, lemonade 273
seafood gumbo 110
shepherd's pie 164
shabu-shabu 183
simple pavlova 246
slice, vanilla 279
smoked ham and pumpkin soup 43
snapper, crumbed 123
soup, smoked ham and pumpkin 43
South African braai (BBQ) 179

spaghetti alla diavola 208
spaghetti sauce 174
spinach and cheese triangles 211
steamed coral trout Thai style 73
stew, veal, with parsley dumplings 199
Straddie pizza 35

T

tarts, caramelised onion and goat's
  cheese 207
tomato paste 35
traditional spaghetti sauce 174
treacle sponge puddings 243
trout see coral trout

U

udon prawn salad 99

V

vanilla slice 279
veal bake, crumbed 202
veal stew with parsley dumplings 199
vegetable pakora 222
vegetable paratha roll 225

W

whole fried fish with two sauces 81

Picture credits

AAP/AP Photo/Mark Baker 86

C. Pierre Tostce 120

Charmaine Dick 5, 6t, 128, 280

Getty Images/Tom Shaw 139

Hamish Blair 40, 41, 152, 181, 212t, 218t, 219, 248

Justin Levitt Photography 118–119, 124–125

Matthew Hayden 6b,10,11,14t,18t, 20l, 24, 28, 33, 44, 50, 60, 71, 74t, 78, 82, 87, 90r, 100b, 108t, 108bl, 113, 117, 132br, 136, 138, 141, 144, 148bl, 152br, 153, 162, 173, 176t, 186, 190, 191, 192t, 200, 201, 212b, 218b, 226, 236, 240, 241, 244, 256, 257, 268, 276

Newspix/Brett Costello 126

Newspix/Colleen Petch 166

Newspix/Lydon Methielson 127

Newspix/Michael Klein 252, 253

Newspix/Phil Hillyard 64, 65, 82, 104, 105, 148t

Newspix/Wayne Dudley 156–157

Paul A. Broben 56–57, 112, 249, 282

Steve Waugh 148br, 220, 252t, 252b

Vincent Long 2–3, 8–9, 14b, 20r, 32, 36, 37, 54–55, 70, 74b, 90l, 100t, 108br, 116, 121, 132t, 140, 145, 158, 159, 176b, 192b, 204–205, 252l, 262

KEY TO LEGEND: t = top, r = right, l = left, b = bottom, br = bottom right, bl = bottom left

The ABC 'Wave' device is a trademark of the
Australian Broadcasting Corporation and is used
under licence by HarperCollins*Publishers* Australia.

First published by ABC Books as two separate books:
The Matthew Hayden Cookbook in 2004, and
The Matthew Hayden Cookbook 2 in 2006

This combined edition first published in Australia in 2009
by HarperCollins*Publishers* Australia Pty Limited
ABN 36 009 913 517
harpercollins.com.au

HarperCollins*Publishers*
25 Ryde Road, Pymble, Sydney, NSW 2073, Australia
31 View Road, Glenfield, Auckland 0627, New Zealand
A 53, Sector 57, Noida, India
77–85 Fulham Palace Road, London W6 8JB, United Kingdom
2 Bloor Street East, 20th floor, Toronto, Ontario M4W 1A8, Canada
10 East 53rd Street, New York NY 10022, USA

National Library of Australia Cataloguing-in-Publication data:

Hayden, Matthew.
The Matthew Hayden complete cookbook / Matthew Hayden.
9780733326202 (pbk.)
Includes index.
Cookery. Cricket players – Australia – Anecdotes.
Australian Broadcasting Corporation.

641.5

Cover photograph by Steve Baccon
Cover design by Darren Holt, HarperCollins Design Studio
Food photography by Andre Martin
Food styling by Jane Collins
Internal design by saso content & design pty ltd
Typeset in EgyptienneF LT 10.5/15 by saso content & design pty ltd
Colour reproduction by Graphic Print Group, Adelaide
Printed and bound in China by RR Donnelley on 128 gsm Matt art

8 7 6 5 4 3   11 12